BLACK HAWK

S.F. TOMAJCZYK

MBI

First published in 2003 by MBI Publishing Company,
Galtier Plaza, Suite 200, 380 Jackson Street, St. Paul,
MN 55101-3885 USA

The information in this book is true and complete to the best
of our knowledge. All recommendations are made without any
guarantee on the part of the author or Publisher, who also
disclaim any liability incurred in connection with the use of
this data or specific details.

We recognize that some words, model names, and designations,
for example, mentioned herein are the property of the
trademark holder. We use them for identification purposes only.
This is not an official publication.

MBI Publishing Company titles are also available at discounts
in bulk quantity for industrial or sales-promotional use.
For details write to Special Sales Manager at Motorbooks
International Wholesalers & Distributors, Galtier Plaza,
Suite 200, 380 Jackson Street, St. Paul,
MN 55101-3885 USA

Library of Congress Cataloging-in-Publication Data

Tomajczyk, Stephen F.
    Black Hawk / by S. F. Tomajczyk.
      p. cm.
    ISBN 0-7603-1591-4 (pbk. : alk. paper)
    1. Black Hawk (Military transport helicopter) I. Title.

UG1232.T72T65 2003
623.7'46047--dc21

On Contents page: U.S. Coast Guard

On the front cover: A U.S. Army Black Hawk helicopter flies a
security mission over southern Turkey to enforce the United
Nations "No Fly" zone north of the 36th parallel. *U.S. Army*

On the frontispiece: Loadmasters aboard a C-17 Globemaster
III cargo plane from the 17th Expeditionary Airlift Squadron
prepare to unload an UH-60L Black Hawk helicopter. All H-60
helicopters have folding rotor blades, which enables them to be
placed aboard aircraft for deployment anywhere in the world.
It takes only a few hours to reassemble the helicopters after
their arrival. *U.S. Air Force*

On the title page: A close-up look at an HH-60H Combat Support
Helicopter flown by HS-2 Golden Falcons as it prepares to deploy
a Navy SEAL squad. An inflatable raft, affixed to the underside of
the fuselage (you can see part of it in the bottom left of this
photo), is dropped first. Then the SEALs jump about 10 feet into
the water, where they retrieve the raft and continue with their
mission. While conducting this insertion, the helicopter's gunner
provides suppressive fire if necessary. *S. F. Tomajczyk*

On the back cover: *Richard Zellner/Sikorsky Aircraft*

About the author: A graduate of the University of Michigan and
the New York Institute of Photography, Steve Tomajczyk is an
author who specializes in military affairs, counterterrorism, and
emergency preparedness. He is the author of 10 books, including
Carrier Battle Group and *U.S. Elite Counterterrorist Forces.* His work
has appeared in a variety of publications and television shows,
including *People* magazine, *NBC Dateline*, and *Extra*. Tomajczyk is
listed in *Who's Who in America* and *Contemporary Authors*, and is
professionally affiliated with the Author's Guild, American Society
of Media Photographers, International Association of Emergency
Managers, and the International Association of Counterterrorism
and Security Professionals. He lives in New Hampshire.

Edited by Amy Glaser
Designed by Brenda Canales

Printed in China

CONTENTS

A KETTLE OF HAWKS

The U.S. Army has a tradition of naming its helicopters after Native American tribes: Iroquois. Kiowa. Apache. When it came time to name the UH-60 helicopter, the service settled on Black Hawk, in reference to the 1832 Black Hawk War. In that conflict, Chief Black Hawk led a band of Sac and Fox Indians back into Illinois after having moved west of the Mississippi. They were attacked—and most were killed—on the Bad Axe River (in present-day Wisconsin) by a force under Henry Atkinson.

Yet the Black Hawk helicopter has more in common with the predatory bird rather than an Indian-related conflict. For instance, hawks ride the warm thermals skyward and then, unexpectedly, turn on a wingtip and zoom to the ground. In the military, Black Hawk helicopters are renowned for their agility, power, and speed. One moment they're soaring through the sky, and the next they're dancing six feet over trees, hills, and power lines while flying the contours of the earth.

Second, there are literally dozens of hawk species in Nature. Hence, a group of hawks—referred to by ornithologists as a kettle of hawks—could theoretically include Cooper's Hawks, Red-Tailed Hawks, Goshawks, Marsh Hawks, Broad-Winged Hawks, and White-Tailed Hawks. Again, the military parallel is intriguing, with its Black Hawk, Pave Hawk, Seahawk, Jayhawk, Whitehawk, and Firehawk. While they are all hawks, each is different

enough to warrant a birdwatcher's guide of distinctive identifying characteristics.

And last, when hawks combat one another midair, they grasp each other's talons and tumble end-over-end toward the ground, screeching and pecking until one gives up or they both slam into the earth. Likewise, the Black Hawk helicopters are not reluctant to battle an enemy. They can be armed tooth and claw with many weapon systems. Better yet, they are intentionally designed to take a hit—actually, a lot of hits!—and keep on fighting.

This book takes an inside look at this amazing helicopter and explores how it has adapted over the past quarter century to perform everything from combat assault to search-and-rescue and from aeromedical evacuation to drug interdiction. It even examines the Black Hawk's role in protecting space shuttle launches and transporting the president of the United States.

The majority of the information included in this book has been obtained from primary sources, such as Sikorsky Aircraft, the U.S. military, and former helicopter pilots. That's because much of the information posted on the Internet is incomplete and, in many instances, incorrect.

Without question, this book would not have been possible without the assistance of the following individuals and organizations who contributed not only their expertise, but also vital information and technical assistance at a time when our country was at war removing Saddam Hussein from power: LCDR Dawn Cutler, U.S.N., Navy Office of Information; LCDR Ed Zeigler, U.S.N., Media Services, Navy Office of Information; LCDR Greg Hicks, U.S.N., Navy Office of Information–East; LCDR David Waterman, U.S.N., Navy Office of Information–East; Christopher J. Madden, Director, Navy Visual News Service; Mike Maus, Public Affairs Specialist, COMNAVAIRLANT; Lt. Wes Hester, U.S.C.G., Air Station Elizabeth City; PA3 Scott Whitney, U.S.C.G., Atlantic Area Public Affairs; CDR Paul Lange, U.S.C.G., Air Station Elizabeth City; GY Sgt. Timothy McGough, U.S.M.C., Public Affairs New York; Capt. Jeff Weymouth, U.S.M.C., Quantico Marine Corps Base; Capt. Jaret Heil, U.S.M.C., XO, Public Affairs New York, Maj. David Andersen, U.S.M.C., director, Public Affairs New York; Capt. Jerome Bryant, U.S.M.C., Media Officer, Quantico MCAB; Maj. Gen. Joseph Bergantz, U.S.A., PEO, Army Aviation; 2d Lt. Anna Siegel, U.S.A.F., Public Affairs Officer, Air Combat Command; Lt. Gabe Johnson, U.S.A.F., Public Affairs Officer, Special Operations Command; Gen. John Blair, Adjutant General, NH National Guard; Lt. Col. Frank Leith, NH National Guard; U.S. Naval Air Systems Command; U.S. Marine Corps Helicopter Squadron One (HMX-1), Executive Flight Detachment; Army Aviation School, Fort Rucker, Alabama; Corpus Christi Army Depot; U.S. Army Aviation and Missile Command; 347th Rescue Wing, U.S.A.F. Air Combat Command; John Grady, Public Affairs, Association of the U.S. Army; and Cynthia Swain, vice-president of Corporate Communications, L-3 Communications.

A warm and special thank you is extended to the folks at Sikorsky Aircraft, most notably William Tuttle, manager of public relations, Richard Zellner, senior photographic illustrator, and Bob Kenney, Naval Hawk program manager.

I especially enjoyed my conversation with Steven Schmidt, who is presently director of program productions at Sikorsky. He was one of the original "kids" who designed the Black Hawk back in the late 1960s, using a slide rule, notepad, and gut instinct—truly an amazing feat when you think about the state-of-the-art technology relied on today to engineer and build aircraft. Talking with him put this entire book into perspective. It was truly an honor to take a peek at the events 30 years ago that resulted in a major revolution in rotary-wing aviation.

—S. F. Tomajczyk
May 2003

CHAPTER ONE

BLACK HAWK

A flight of two Black Hawks on a training exercise. Survivability features of these helicopters include self-sealing fuel tanks, triple redundant hydraulic and electrical systems, wire cutters, jettisonable cockpit doors, energy-absorbing landing gear, and a fuselage and rotor blade system that can withstand hits from 23mm ammunition. *Richard Zellner/Sikorsky Aircraft*

Upon first consideration, the helicopter is not an ideal military platform. It is noisy. It vibrates. It thirsts for fuel and requires a lot of maintenance. Its rotor blades are vulnerable to small-arms fire, and it is slower than its fixed-wing counterparts. For these reasons, the helicopter was relegated mainly to medical evacuation and search-and-rescue missions in the decades following World War II.

It was not until the Vietnam War that the concept of air cavalry reached full maturity. During that conflict, the mountainous and tropical-like environment prevented the U.S. military from easily moving its soldiers and combat equipment to fight the Viet Cong. The roads were unpaved and often muddy, which caused tanks, trucks, and towed howitzers to bog down. Similarly, the jungles slowed the progress of soldiers and prevented them from seeing booby traps and enemy forces.

To address this issue, the Pentagon tried using the Bell UH-1 Huey (which was rarely called by its official name, Iroquois) for combat air assault purposes. The concept, tested and refined by Lieutenant Colonel Hal Moore, entailed having armed soldiers ride the helicopter onto the battlefield to fight the Viet Cong and then quickly hopscotch back out to safety.

The tactic worked quite well, and the helicopter was subsequently integrated into the military's land-warfare doctrine. Now the helicopter would be used not just for evacuation and search-and-rescue but also for combat air assault, external lift, reconnaissance, command and control, electronic warfare, and special operations.

The only problem was that the venerable Huey was not capable of assuming all these roles. So the army, in the late 1960s, began conducting surveys to determine what design features the next helicopter should embrace. They focused on the warrant officers and flight officers who actually flew the Huey in combat and asked, "How do we improve the Huey? What can we do to save soldiers in the helicopter and make it the best helicopter for the battlefield?"

The answers they received helped the army establish the criteria for what eventually became known as the Utility Tactical Transport Aircraft System (UTTAS).

Among the requirements were;

Power. Without question, the pilots wanted a helicopter that was over-powered. They wanted their helicopter to offer the same performance on a hot, 95-degree day at 4,000 feet as it did at sea level on a typical day. When the army looked at a map of the world, they realized that future wars would be fought within this 4,000-foot/95-degree constraint—conditions that rob a helicopter of its lift—so they made high power a design requirement.

Speed and stealth. The ability to travel quickly over the battlefield and insert/extract soldiers means less vulnerability, so the army requested that the UTTAS be faster than the Huey and that it be able to fly close to the earth. The helicopter also had to be quiet, so enemy forces would not hear it coming. This was important because the Huey made a distinctive "whop whop" noise—a result of the advancing side of the rotor tips reaching supersonic speed and creating small shock waves. The Viet Cong often heard an approaching Huey miles away, giving them time to grab their weapons.

An Army National Guard Staff Sergeant conducts routine maintenance on the tail rotor of a UH-60Q Black Hawk used for medical evacuation. Retractable steps and recessed handholds in the tail assembly provide easy access to work areas. *Department of Defense*

Maneuverability. To avoid enemy anti-aircraft missiles and ground fire, a helicopter must be able to fly low and fast. The army asked that the UTTAS be agile enough to climb quickly, to clear hills and obstacles when flying nap-of-the-earth, and then almost immediately dive back down. And it had to do so while its airframe and rotors withstood the high, instantaneous G-forces caused by such abrupt maneuvers.

Size. Small helicopters make small targets. Hence, the UTTAS needed to be of a size that enabled soldiers to quickly and safely embark/ disembark. Also, it had to fit inside a C-130 Hercules for transport overseas.

Survivability. Many Hueys were shot down by small-arms fire in Vietnam, so the army required that the next-generation helicopter be able to fly for 30 minutes after sustaining a hit anywhere in the underside and lower fuselage by a 7.62mm bullet fired from a range of just 300 feet. Additionally, they wanted to make certain that no fire would occur if the helicopter crashed or was struck by a large-caliber round.

After the Request for Proposal went out in January 1972 for UTTAS, the field of contenders was narrowed down to the Boeing Vertol YUH-61A and the Sikorsky YUH-60A, each powered by a pair of specially designed General Electric engines. Both companies received contracts in August 1972 to build three prototypes of their helicopter designs for competitive evaluation by the army.

In December 1976, just two days before Christmas, the army announced that the Sikorsky-designed helicopter was superior and that it would proceed with low-rate production to make any final modifications before gearing up with full production.

What caught the army's attention was that the Sikorsky design not only met all the UTTAS requirements (not every submission did) but in many instances far exceeded them.

For instance, where survivability issues were concerned, the helicopter had redundant tail rotor controls, redundant control systems, and triple-redundant hydraulic and electrical systems. These multiple backups enabled the helicopter to keep flying even if it suffered severe battle damage.

Additionally, the helicopter's revolutionary fuel tank was self-sealing, meaning it could be hit by anything up to .50-caliber ammunition without explosion, fire, or leakage. Likewise, the entire fuselage and the composite titanium/fiberglass rotor blades could take a hit from 23mm weapons fire without serious damage. To survive a crash the helicopter was equipped with high-energy landing gear to absorb the shock of a 30-foot-per-second rate of fall, and the entire airframe was designed to progressively crush on impact to protect the passengers.

The army began fielding the UH-60A Black Hawk—all army helicopters are named after Native American tribes—in 1979. The first unit to be equipped with it was the 101st Airborne Division at Fort Campbell, Kentucky. Today, six Black Hawk helicopter models are in service: the UH-60A and UH-60L for general combat support, the UH-60Q for medical evacuation, the EH-60 for electronic warfare, and the MH-60L and MH-60K for special operations.

Combat Support Helicopters

The army procured more than 900 UH-60A model helicopters, replacing the UH-1 Huey in air support,

UH-60L Specifications

Crew: Three—two pilots and a crew chief
Length: 64 feet, 10 inches
Height: 17 feet, 6 inches
Rotor diameter: 53 feet, 9 inches
Maximum takeoff weight: 23,500 pounds (with external load)
Engines: Two General Electric T700-GE-701C engines, each rated at 1,890 shp
Speed: 184 mph cruise (225 mph maximum)
External cargo load: 9,000 pounds
Range: 285 statute miles, flying at 4,000 feet at 150 mph with a 20-minute reserve. If two 230-gallon external tanks are added, the range is increased to 680 miles.
Fuel tanks: One 360-gallon internal tank; two optional 230- or 450-gallon external tanks.
Ceiling: 19,100 feet
Weapons: Two 7.62mm machine guns, 7.62mm miniguns (six-barreled) or .50-caliber miniguns (three-barreled) mounted in the cabin windows. The External Stores Support System (ESSS) can be affixed to deploy additional weapon systems, including 70mm aerial rockets, AGM-114 Hellfire laser-guided missiles, air-to-air Stinger missiles, a 7.62mm gun pod, 20mm gun pod, and 30mm chain gun.
Unit cost: $5.9 million

airmobile cavalry, and air ambulance units. The Black Hawk is a twin-engine, single-rotor, four-bladed utility helicopter powered by two T700-GE-700 turboshafts, each producing 1,560 shp. General Electric designed the engines for minimum maintenance in harsh environments—such as the desert—and to resist small-caliber bullets. Maintenance is accomplished in part with a self-contained lubrication system and a built-in inlet particle separator.

In addition to the survivability characteristics mentioned previously, the Black Hawk features a hydraulically adjusted tailplane (also known as a stabilator) for low-speed maneuvers and to improve control during nap-of-the-earth flying and assault operations. Other protective features include cockpit displays compatible with night-vision goggles, which permits flying the helicopter at night; ballistic seats for the pilot and copilot; low-reflective paint; and infrared suppressors on the engine and oil-cooler exhaust systems to deter heat-seeking missiles.

The helicopter's fixed tailwheel is intentionally positioned at the rear of the tail pylon, to assist with roll-

Litter bearers unload a simulated patient off a UH-60Q Black Hawk MEDEVAC helicopter. A dedicated medical package can be installed in the large cabin of these helicopters, essentially turning them into flying ambulances. It features supports for six litters, patient lighting, five intensive-care stations, an oxygen generating system, a medical suction system, a medical storage cabinet, and seating for three attendants. *Department of Defense*

War can occur in any environment, even in the far-flung frozen regions of the world. As a result, the military must train and be ready to fight in those wastelands. In this photograph, UH-60L Black Hawk helicopters (although Frozen Hawk might be more appropriate) wearing skis prepare for an air-assault training mission on the fictional town of Simpsonville in the Yukon Training Area near Fort Greely, Alaska. *Department of Defense*

on landings if the tail rotor is lost. It also allows the pilot to make aggressive landings in confined spaces, such as a forest clearing or the roof of a building. Approaching in a high flare position, the pilot slams the tailwheel onto the ground and then uses it as a pivot point to rotate the rest of the helicopter into the landing zone.

To thwart missiles, the Black Hawk is equipped with a radar warning receiver as well as the M-130 General Purpose Dispenser, which launches either 30 decoy flares or 30 chaff cartridges. Chaff is an antiradar countermeasure consisting of extremely thin (i.e., 0.1mm-diameter) aluminized glass fibers or silvered nylon fibers that are dispensed in bundles from the aircraft. When the bundle bursts open, it forms a compact, reflective cloud of suspended fibers that creates false radar targets and breaks the lock of the incoming missile's tracking-radar system.

Many UH-60A Black Hawks also carry the ALQ-144 Countermeasures Set. Affixed to the oil cooler-exhaust (just rear of the main rotor), the system protects the helicopter from heat-seeking missiles by automatically jamming or confusing the missile's infrared sensor. The ALQ-144 is easily identified on helicopters by its cylindrical shape, which is covered with what appears to be small mirrors. In fact, due to its appearance, most aviators refer to it as the disco light.

Up, up, and away! UH-60L Black Hawk helicopters lift off at Cairo West Air Base in Egypt during Exercise Bright Star, a yearly tactical field exercise. Although five helicopters are shown taking off simultaneously, they are actually organized into flights (formations) of two aircraft. That's because flights of three or more helicopters are slower, more unwieldy, and more difficult to control, which is dangerous when defensive maneuvers must be taken quickly. Every formation has a flight lead (who navigates the way to the objective while avoiding obstacles and threats) and a wingman (who has visual lookout and radar responsibilities and performs backup navigation tasks). *Department of Defense*

The Black Hawk is designed to carry an 11-man, fully equipped infantry squad into battle in most weather conditions, while flying low and fast. When exiting the cabin by way of the two doors on either side, the soldiers do so hunched over. That's because the cabin, while fairly large, is only 54 inches high.

The helicopter's crew chief mans one of the two 7.62mm machine guns mounted in the cabin's forward windows, providing suppressive cover fire when necessary. The other machine gun can be fired by one of the infantry soldiers when approaching a hot landing zone. This offers some protection to both sides of the helicopter.

The UH-60A not only flies faster than the antiquated UH-1 Huey—nearly twice as fast—but does so with more payload. Fifteen Black Hawks can accomplish the same amount of work as 23 Hueys.

One creative use of its external cargo hook—besides transporting a Humvee and other combat gear—is to sling a 105mm howitzer beneath a Black Hawk and fly it, its crew of six, and 30 rounds of ammunition to a location where the crew sets up and fires a round at a target. Then, just as quickly, they jump back onto the helicopter and dash to another location before the enemy can react.

The Black Hawk's maneuverability has changed the face of warfare. Today, combat is not only fluid and fast, it can now inflict more uncertainty and surprise on enemy forces.

In October 1989, the army began upgrading the Black Hawk's two T700-GE-700 engines to the T700-GE-701C turboshaft and added a more durable gearbox. At 1,890 shp, the engine is not only 24 percent more powerful than its predecessor but provides greater lifting capacity, improved corrosion protection, and better high-altitude and hot-weather performance.

As a result of these modifications, the army decided to designate it as a new model—the UH-60L Black Hawk. To date, more than 500 have been fielded.

While horsepower is important, so is firepower. This is why the UH-60L began trading its window-mounted M60 7.62mm machine guns for more deadly, six-barreled 7.62mm miniguns or three-barreled .50-caliber miniguns—both capable of firing 4,000 rounds per minute. The new Black Hawk also heralded the use of the External Stores Support System (ESSS), to expand its battlefield capabilities.

The ESSS is comprised of four external pylons from which a variety of fuel and weapon-system options

Flight simulation is a safe and effective way to hone the skills of pilots as well as prepare them for specific missions by using geographical databases that display the terrain they will encounter. This photo shows just one of six reconfigurable, interactive cockpit simulators found in an AVCATT (Aviation Combined Arms Tactical Trainer) suite, which are housed in two 53-foot-long trailers. The helmet-mounted displays replicate a wide range of combat and environmental conditions, such as battlefield smoke; weapons effects; blowing snow, dust, or sand; and variances in wind, visibility, and cloud ceiling. They can be imitated under day, dusk, or night environments. *L-3 Communications*

guided Hellfire anti-armor missiles (4 per launcher), an SUU-25 flare launcher, air-to-air Stinger missiles (2 per launcher), 20mm cannon pods, and a 30mm chain gun. The type of weapons actually hung on one of the four pylons is determined by the combat mission and, of course, availability.

One of the more unusual roles the Black Hawk fulfills is that of an airborne mine layer, using the M139 Air Volcano mine-dispensing system affixed to the exterior. In a mere 17 seconds, the helicopter can launch 960 mines, creating two instant minefields. Their size is determined by the helicopter's altitude and speed but can measure up to 3,000 by 360 feet. These serve to delay or halt an enemy force or to deny the use of a vital asset, such as an air field.

Two Air Volcano racks, each comprised of 40 canisters, are attached to both sides of the Black Hawk, near its cabin doors. Each canister holds five antitank mines and one antipersonnel mine. The Volcano operator aboard the helicopter controls the rate at which the mines are sown and their self-destruct time (4 hours, 48 hours, or 15 days), to protect civilians and advancing friendly troops from potential harm. The system can be reloaded with new munitions in about 20 minutes, allowing the helicopter to return to the battlefield soon.

Air Ambulance

One of the realities of war is that soldiers are wounded and killed on the battlefield. Operations Just Cause and Desert Storm demonstrated how important it was to get the wounded to a hospital as quickly as possible—preferably during the golden hour just after being wounded—to improve their chances of survival. To facilitate this, the army turned the Black

can be mounted. The outboard pylons carry 1,650 pounds each; the inboard pylons, 3,160 pounds. When 230- and 450-gallon auxiliary fuel tanks are hung from these pylons, the Black Hawk's range is increased to 1,380 miles.

As for armaments, the ESSS can be configured with a mix of 70mm aerial rockets (19 per pod), laser-

A sight that gives enemy forces the jitters: a formation of six Black Hawk helicopters speeding toward them. When a large number of helicopters are used for a mission, they are broken down into two-ship elements. The spacing between aircraft is determined by the threat, terrain, illumination, weather conditions, and the capabilities of the crews and aircraft in the flight. Generally, the greater the threat, the looser and smaller the formation, since it is more difficult to detect. By contrast, the rougher the terrain and the lower the visibility, the tighter and smaller the formation should be. *U.S. Army*

Hawk into a modern air ambulance by installing a state-of-the-art medical interior that accommodates up to six acute-care patients and three attendants.

Designated the UH-60Q Black Hawk MEDEVAC helicopter, it is essentially a miniature trauma center that delivers patient care while flying faster and further than the older UH-60A helos. The interior layout was designed by Air Methods Inc., which relied on ergonomic design to maximize the helicopter's cabin space, placing sophisticated, life-saving equipment at the medics' fingertips. The helicopter is equipped with patient monitoring equipment, an oxygen generating system, airway management and suction systems, medical equipment, a medical storage cabinet, and five intensive-care stations. The entire interior has night-vision-goggle-compatible lighting, which enables medics to provide trauma care when the helicopter is behind enemy lines and all white light must be turned off.

In addition to providing battlefield evacuation in all weather conditions, the UH-60Q is able to assist with combat search-and-rescue (it has an external rescue hoist), forward surgical team transport, hospital ship lifeline missions, medical logistics resupply, and humanitarian relief missions. The helicopter has digital communications and is equipped with an integrated Doppler Radar/GPS navigation system, a Personnel Locator System, and Forward-Looking Infrared (FLIR), which enables the pilots to fly at night. FLIR sees things in the dark and displays them on a screen the pilot constantly monitors, enabling him to fly fast and low without crashing. (Older helo models, some of which double as unofficial air ambulances, do not have FLIR.)

Electronic Warfare

As army generals H. Norman Schwarzkopf and Tommy Franks can readily attest, possessing timely and accurate military intelligence can mean the difference between winning or losing a battle. Knowing where the enemy is located and what assets he has—and how he has arranged them—can provide the key on how to defeat them.

In the past, combat leaders relied on binoculars and eyewitness reports, but in today's world, the military focuses on the electromagnetic spectrum—which encompasses everything from infrared to ultraviolet light and from radar to radio waves. That's because nearly everything on the battlefield emits an electronic signal in this spectrum. For instance, voice communication systems operated by soldiers, tanks, and other combat assets use HF, VHF, and SHF radio frequencies. Weapon aiming systems use radar or microwave frequencies. Heat-seeking missiles use infrared.

Electronically speaking, the battlefield is deafening. By vacuuming the signals being transmitted and classifying them, a military commander can map the entire battlefield—right down to the types of weapons being deployed, and where. Knowing this, he can then respond with an appropriate plan of attack or jam the enemy's frequencies to deny him vital information.

Collectively, this is known as electronic warfare, and it is the job of the EH-60 Quick Fix helicopter. Since its

Soldiers hustle aboard Black Hawk helicopters in a landing zone during a field exercise. The helicopter features a flexible internal cabin arrangement that can be configured for search-and-rescue, casualty evacuation, and, as in this case, troop transport. The Black Hawk can seat 12 to 20 troops. *U.S. Army*

The UH-60Q Black Hawk MEDEVAC helicopter can accommodate three to six acute-care patients and their medical attendants. Ergonomic design has maximized the cabin space, enabling sophisticated lifesaving equipment to be deployed into combat, thereby improving the chances of saving a wounded soldier's life. *Sikorsky Aircraft*

introduction in 1988, there have been several models of the Quick Fix, including the EH-60A Quick Fix II, EH-60B SOTAS, EH-60C Command and Control Aircraft, and the EH-60L Advanced Quick Fix. Although the exact capabilities of these helicopters are classified, they are easily distinguished from other Black Hawk models by the many dipole antenna arrays mounted on their fuselage as well as a retractable aerial extending from the underfuselage.

Quick Fix is the codename for an electronic countermeasures system that intercepts, locates, and jams enemy communications. It had been installed earlier on modified UH-1 Huey helicopters and was moved to the UH-60A Black Hawk, which has has greater range, speed, and endurance. It can also hold more equipment, which bodes well for future advancements in electronic warfare.

The army calls this version Quick Fix II and acquired 66 of them, placing them with air assault divisions and military intelligence battalions. It is capable of intercepting a signal, determining its source using onboard direction-finding equipment, and then jamming it from as far away as 18 miles. The helicopter has a crew of four: two pilots and two electronic warfare (EW) technicians.

The follow-on to the EH-60A Quick Fix II was the EH-60B Stand-Off Target Acquisition System (SOTAS), which was designed to provide a "God's-eye view" of the battlefield by tracking and classifying moving targets (e.g., tanks, vehicles) and then transmitting the information to army ground stations. Its search-radar antenna was mounted inside a rectangular tube under the fuselage; the antenna could be lowered and rotated as necessary to detect ground targets.

Only one EH-60B SOTAS helicopter was built before the project was absorbed by the air force in 1982. An improved version of SOTAS later evolved into JSTARS—the Joint Surveillance and Target Attack Radar System—used today by E-8 Joint STARS aircraft to provide commanders with wide-area surveillance and deep-targeting data on targets day or night, in all weather conditions.

The EH-60C Quick Fix IIB is an airborne tactical command post that is presently being explored. It is a Black Hawk helicopter equipped with large-screen displays, advanced voice and data communications, and five interchangeable workstations for the commander, intelligence officer, operations officer, fire support officer, and one other staff officer.

The army envisions this helicopter patrolling the skies near a battlefield to enhance the commander's ability to wage war. It will provide greater situational awareness of what is happening on the battlefield, using digital maps and data from E-8 JSTARS, unmanned aerial vehicles such as the Predator, and close-air support aircraft such as the A-10 Thunderbolt. Based on this, the commander can adjust his plans and military forces accordingly.

Two prototype EH-60C helicopters have been deployed with the 4th Infantry Division for testing. It is expected that the EH-60C will be fielded to the 1st Cavalry Division in 2005 and to III Corps in 2006.

The most current EW helicopter is the EH-60L Advanced Quick Fix (AQF). The system is mounted on a UH-60L Black Hawk, which, of course, features the more powerful 701C GE turboshaft engines, improved flight controls, and upgraded radio communications, compared to its older EH-60A cousin. The airframe was modified to accept the AQF mission equipment as well as two external fuel tanks to increase its endurance to four hours, an upgraded Inertial Navigational System, and an environmental control system.

While Quick Fix II can locate and intercept VHF and UHF frequencies, AQF is capable of detecting, direction finding, identifying, and tracking communication signals

The advanced digital (also known as "glass") cockpit provides the pilot and copilot each with two active-matrix, liquid-crystal screens—a flight display and a mission display. The flight display has all the primary flight instruments compressed into less than a square foot, making it easier for the pilot to scan everything. The mission display enables him to scroll to different functions, such as color weather radar, FLIR, and a moving digital map. The glass cockpit is intended to reduce cockpit clutter and the aircrew's workload. *Sikorsky Aircraft*

Soldiers establish a protective perimeter around a landing zone for two incoming Black Hawk helicopters assigned to the Hawaii National Guard. After landing, the soldiers will mount the helicopters in a fast but orderly manner, with the Black Hawk gunner providing suppressive fire as necessary. *Richard Zellner/Sikorsky Aircraft*

in the HF, UHF, VHF, and SHF frequency bands, as well as several satellite communication bands. This enables commanders to precisely locate enemy forces and determine their intentions by electronically mapping the battlefield.

Initially, 32 EH-60A Quick Fix II helicopters were supposed to have been upgraded to the EH-60L AQF model, but due to budget constraints, the army decided to fund only four for testing. As of this writing, the program is still in limbo, with officials wondering whether to adopt the Advanced Quick Fix or switch to an electronic warfare program codenamed Prophet.

Special Operations

One last important Black Hawk helicopter mission is the insertion, resupply, reinforcement, and extraction of special-operations forces (e.g., Green Berets, Rangers, Delta Force) deep behind enemy lines, under adverse weather conditions at night. This is accomplished by the 160th Special Operations Aviation Regiment (SOAR) (also known as Night Stalkers), which flies modified MH-60L and MH-60K helicopters—among other aircraft.

The 160th SOAR was created in 1981 after the failed April 1980 rescue attempt of U.S. Embassy personnel in Teheran. The after-mission review pointed out that helicopter operations needed restructuring for future covert operations. The unit was subsequently tasked with developing air tactics in support of special-operations missions.

The 160th SOAR is nicknamed the Night Stalkers because most of its missions take place under cover of darkness. Many of the unit's pilots have logged 2,000-plus flight hours wearing night-vision goggles—

The MH-60K is a modified UH-60L Black Hawk flown by the 160th Special Operations Aviation Regiment (Nightstalkers) to insert, extract, and resupply Green Berets, Delta Force, and other special-operations forces. *Richard Zellner/Sikorsky Aircraft*

This special operations MH-60K Black Hawk features two auxiliary fuel tanks on its External Fuel Support pods, enabling the helicopter to fly more than 750 miles without refueling. This kind of range is often necessary when inserting or extracting special-operations forces in hostile territory. The placement of the tanks enables the gunner to provide suppressive fire without severe limitations. *Richard Zellner/Sikorsky Aircraft*

gaining a neck size or two in the process from the NVGs' weight. The pilots, all volunteers, are known for their ability to perform bold and dangerous aerial maneuvers; they take pride in venturing into situations where few dare tread.

The public was unaware of the 160th SOAR until October 1983, when the unit conducted an air assault against the Richmond Hill prison, on the island nation of Grenada, as part of Operation Urgent Fury. After coming under heavy fire, the first attempt was aborted. A second assault, however, managed to land the ground force. The two attempts to land on the prison resulted in extensive damage to all six Black Hawks. Civilian film footage showed one of these helicopters crashing east of Salines Airfield as a result of its battle damage.

In 1993, Night Stalker pilot CWO Michael Durant was shot down by militiamen in Mogadishu, Somalia, while searching for warlord Mohammed Fahra Aideed.

Two soldiers lug their combat gear to a waiting Black Hawk helicopter. Dusty environments, such as the desert, can reduce a pilot's visibility and cause spatial disorientation. As for the helicopter itself, it was designed to work in these harsh environments and is equipped with special filters to trap the dirt, so it doesn't damage the twin engines. *Richard Zellner/Sikorsky Aircraft*

Durant's Black Hawk helicopter and another Black Hawk were both hit by rocket-propelled grenades while attempting to insert special-operations forces. His 11-day capture ordeal, which served as the basis for the best-selling book and movie *Black Hawk Down*, inadvertently brought the covert unit to the world's attention once again.

The first Black Hawk helicopter model the 160th SOAR flew in the early 1980s was the UH-60A—which they redesignated the MH-60A. These were among the first army helicopters to be tricked out with a FLIR sensor and the disco light infrared jammer. They also received radar-warning receivers,

satellite communications, hover infrared-suppressor system, M134 7.62mm miniguns, and two 172-gallon Guardian auxiliary fuel tanks that doubled the helicopter's flight time.

Several years later, the MH-60L Black Hawk model was introduced as an interim low-end, special-operations helicopter, while the 160th SOAR awaited the arrival of the more sophisticated MH-60K. The MH-60L was partly through its operational evaluation when Iraq invaded Kuwait in 1990. This event accelerated the deployment of the MH-60L; several helicopters served in Desert Shield and Desert Storm, alongside the MH-60A models.

The Special Purpose Insertion and Extraction (SPIE) rig is used to quickly insert or extract special-operations forces in hostile environments. It consists of a rope suspended from the cargo hook of a helicopter, to which the soldiers hitch themselves (usually in pairs) with safety harnesses. They remain suspended below the helicopter for the duration of the flight, their arms extended like wing foils to prevent spinning. In this photo, the SPIE rig is being used by Navy Explosive Ordnance Disposal technicians. *Department of Defense*

The Sikorsky assembly plant in Connecticut is the birthplace of the Black Hawk helicopter. If you look closely, you can see a number of helicopters in various stages of production. Different helicopter sections (e.g., cockpit, tailcone, main rotor pylon) are built separately, then brought together and joined to create the fuselage. Then the engines, electronics, landing gear, flight controls, and so on are added to complete the helicopter. How long does this take? The production and final assembly time alone for a UH-60L is 24 workdays, but that figure doesn't include the weeks or even months it takes to make some of the subassemblies. *Richard Zellner/Sikorsky Aircraft*

In addition to the combat systems found on the MH-60A, the MH-60L "Velcro Hawk"—so named because Night Stalker pilots stick just about anything on it to meet their needs—features the more powerful 701C GE turboshaft engines, increased Kevlar ballistic armor, an external rescue hoist, and ESSS pylons for attaching auxiliary fuel tanks and additional weapon systems. At least 10 of the 37 MH-60L models the 160th SOAR has today have been equipped with an in-flight refueling probe.

New navigation features include a color weather radar system, improved terrain-following/terrain-avoidance radar, and a personnel locator system. The helicopter is also equipped with the Aesop FLIR, an infrared sensor with a built-in laser rangefinder and

The powerful downwash from the rotor blades of a UH-60Q Black Hawk MEDEVAC helicopter forms a crop circle in this tall grass. The helo is equipped with two external fuel tanks to give it additional range, a necessity for search-and-rescue missions.
Richard Zellner/Sikorsky Aircraft

A crew member of an UH-60A Black Hawk prepares for liftoff during Exercise Northern Edge 2003, Alaska's premier joint training exercise, designed to enhance interoperability among the armed forces. More than 1,600 military personnel participated in the exercise. The high-visibility orange exposure suits are to protect the flight crew from the cold weather while ensuring they can be quickly and easily spotted if their helicopter crashes. The color orange stands out against the snow, rocks, and trees. *U.S. Army*

designator. It enables the crew to attack targets at long distances using the laser-guided Hellfire missile.

As a result of the October 7, 1985, hijacking of the Italian cruise ship *Achille Lauro* in the Mediterranean by Palestinian terrorists—in which the American Leon Klinghoffer was killed—the army added a folding tail and stabilator to the MH-60L to ease shipboard use. This was in anticipation of potentially having to conduct sea-based combat and counterterrorism missions in the future.

As for the MH-60K, which entered service in 1995, it is the current top-of-the-line special-operations medium-lift helicopter. Input from a number of Night Stalker pilots resulted in design changes to facilitate long-range missions involving nap-of-the-earth flying at night (and in adverse weather conditions) in close formation with other helicopters.

Nap-of-the-earth flying involves flying as close to the ground as possible, making it difficult for enemy radar to detect the helicopter. The pilot must maintain

A California National Guard Black Hawk helicopter drops a load of water on a wildfire. The water bucket (also known as a Bambi bucket) holds 700 gallons of water and is quickly refilled when the helicopter hovers over a lake or other water source. Sikorsky Aircraft has since developed the Firehawk, a Black Hawk–variant helicopter designed to fight fires and to deploy and recover firefighters. A 1,000-gallon water tank is affixed to the Firehawk's belly. It can be refilled by a snorkel hose in about 60 seconds. *U.S. Army*

a constant low altitude (50 feet or less) and follow the contours of the terrain while simultaneously avoiding obstacles, such as trees and telephone wires. It is a dangerous tactic that does not suffer mistakes. A pilot who loses his attention for a split second can end up plowing into the ground before he realizes it.

The MH-60K helicopter, which can carry 12 soldiers over 750 miles without refueling, features a fully integrated NVG-compatible digital cockpit, a mission management system, an in-flight refueling probe, two removable 230-gallon external fuel tanks, and two miniguns. A new avionics suite includes multi-function displays, FLIR, a digital color-map generator, and terrain-voidance/terrain-following multimode radar. Combined, these enable the pilot to navigate with pinpoint accuracy in all environments and under the harshest of conditions.

At the time of this writing, the army is upgrading the MH-60K once again, to ensure it is capable of infiltrating hostile territory to conduct unconventional warfare and deep reconnaissance missions against terrorists, insurgents, and trained military forces. Some of the modifications include

- An inert-gas generation system that replaces oxygen with nitrogen in the fuel tanks, making them less likely to explode if hit by weapons fire
- A nuclear, biological, and chemical (NBC) crew-protection system

- Lightweight, high-performance wiring that is less vulnerable to electromagnetic energy, so the helicopter can operate around naval ships
- The Special Operations Forces Planning and Rehearsal System, which will provide automatic, near-time mission planning
- Active Noise Reduction in aircrew helmets and headsets, to reduce high noise levels that cause irritability, fatigue, and dizziness
- Condor, a secure, worldwide cellular phone service
- An integrated infrared countermeasures system

Both the MH-60L and MH-60K can be flown worldwide by C-17 Globemaster III, C-5 Galaxy, and C-141 StarLifter aircraft. A maximum of six helicopters can be loaded aboard a Galaxy, while four can be loaded on a Globemaster. It takes an hour to prepare the Black Hawks for loading and another hour to reassemble them at their destination.

In addition to performing covert missions, the MH-60L and MH-60K can conduct strategic intelligence strikes, rapid deployment of troops, combat search-and-rescue, and air assaults. With such a lethal mix of weapons, precision navigation, and advanced avionics, it is no wonder the Night Stalkers' unit patch states "Death Waits in the Dark."

This Black Hawk is equipped with the External Stores Support System, which allows the helicopter to be configured with a variety of auxiliary fuel and weapon system options. The outboard stations have 1,650-pound capacity; the capacity for the inboard stations is 3,160 pounds. In this photo, the helicopter is carrying eight laser-guided AGM-114 Hellfire missiles mounted in clusters of four on the inboard stations, and four Air-to-Air Stinger (ATAS) missiles, two on each outboard station. *Sikorsky Aircraft*

CHAPTER TWO

PAVE HAWK

The Pave Hawk is tasked not only with conducting combat search-and-rescue missions but with inserting, extracting, and resupplying special-operations forces—day or night and in all weather conditions. In this photo, the Pave Hawk is armed with two 7.62mm machine guns. All Pave Hawks are equipped with folding rotor blades and a folding tail stabilator, for shipboard operations and to ease air transportability. *Richard Zellner/Sikorsky Aircraft*

Special Operations

When people see these words, they immediately think of the Army's Green Berets or the Navy's SEAL Teams. Rarely is their first thought the Air Force. Yet, ironically, the Air Force is more involved with special operations than any other military service. Its Combat Control Teams, for instance, are covertly inserted into enemy territory to establish air assault landing zones and close air support for strike aircraft and tactical gunship missions. Its Pararescue jumpers go behind enemy lines to rescue downed aviators and provide trauma care for injured personnel. Its Special Operations Wing uses specially designed aircraft to insert, extract, and resupply special-operations forces (SOF) anywhere in the world, at any time.

Since 1982, when it was first deployed with the Air Force, the Pave Hawk helicopter has played a vital role in all these missions. Today, the Air Force has two versions of the Pave Hawk sitting on its flight lines: the HH-60G, a combat search-and-rescue helicopter, and the MH-60G, a special-operations helicopter.

Combat Search-and-Rescue (CSAR)

The air force is America's lead service for combat search-and-rescue. To fulfill that role, rescue squadrons within the Combat Air Forces use the HH-60G Pave Hawk to recover downed pilots (or other isolated personnel) in up to a medium-threat wartime environment, day or night. But because of its versatility, the Pave Hawk is also often tasked with missions that have nothing to do with combat, such as civil search-and-rescue, aeromedical evacuation, disaster relief, and NASA space shuttle support.

The helicopter is a modified UH-60L Black Hawk and features an upgraded communications and navigation suite. That's because the Pave Hawk is expected to fly extended missions behind enemy lines—just a few feet above the ground, often at night. Without good communications or navigation, it would never reach its destination. Hence, the Pave Hawk has integrated Inertial avigation/GPS/Doppler navigation systems, satellite communications, and Have Quick communications. Have Quick is the codename for a VHF/UHF–band radio system that cannot be easily jammed.

Additionally, all HH-60Gs have an automatic flight-control system, night-vision-goggle-compatible lighting,

HH-60G Specifications

Crew: Five—two pilots, a flight engineer, and two pararescuemen
Length: 64 feet, 9 inches
Height: 16 feet, 9 inches
Rotor diameter: 53 feet, 9 inches
Maximum takeoff weight: 22,500 pounds
Engines: Two General Electric T700-G-700 or T700-FE-701C engines
Speed: 184 mph cruise (220 mph maximum)
Range: 445 statute miles (unlimited with aerial refueling)
Ceiling: 19,000 feet
Active force inventory: 64
Weapons: Two 7.62mm machine guns
Unit cost: $9.3 million (1998 dollars)

A Pave Hawk pilot's view of an MC-130E Combat Talon I special-operations aircraft that is ready to conduct an aerial refueling mission at night. Wearing night-vision goggles, the helicopter's pilot, copilot, and flight engineer will have to work together to carefully match the 125 mph speed and direction of the Combat Talon while inserting the Pave Hawk's extended refueling probe into the basket without cutting the hose with the rotor blades. It takes about 10 minutes to conduct this potentially dangerous 125 mph aerial-refueling dance. *U.S. Air Force*

a retractable in-flight refueling probe, internal auxiliary fuel tanks, and FLIR, which significantly enhances night-time flying. A color weather radar and an anti-icing system for the engine and rotor blades enable the Pave Hawk to fly in adverse weather conditions. That's important, because rescue forces can't wait for a clear, sunny day to recover a downed pilot fleeing enemy soldiers.

For limited self-protection from enemy weapons fire, the HH-60G is armed with two 7.62mm machine guns. It is also equipped with a radar warning receiver, which alerts the crew to radar-homing missiles and to antiaircraft artillery units on the ground that are using radar to aim their guns at them.

To avoid heat-seeking missiles, the Pave Hawk is outfitted with an infrared jammer and a hover infrared suppressor system. The latter plays a key role in significantly reducing the helicopter's infrared (heat) signature when it is in a hover and, therefore, a sitting duck for hostile weapons fire. The Pave Hawk is also painted on the outside with a special, infrared-

Two Air Force combat controllers begin setting up communications equipment after being inserted by an MH-60G Pave Hawk helicopter. Combat controllers serve as the "tip of the spear" by arriving well ahead of the main airborne assault forces in enemy territory to conduct surveillance, establish landing and drop zones, and/or set up air-traffic control systems. *U.S. Air Force*

absorbing paint to make the helicopter less visible to an incoming missile's sensors.

If a missile should somehow get by all these defenses, the HH-60G has a flare/chaff countermeasure dispensing system. The hot-burning flare and expanding cloud of aluminized glass fibers effectively blind the missile, thereby allowing the Pave Hawk to take evasive action and escape.

To rescue a downed pilot, the Pave Hawk either lands or hovers in place and uses a rope ladder or its

Two ghostlike HH-60G Pave Hawk helicopters from the 66th Expeditionary Rescue Squadron take off from an air field to conduct an extraction mission in support of Operation Enduring Freedom. Extracting soldiers from the ground can be accomplished by landing or by using the rescue hoist or ladder. Such missions are always done in pairs, so one helicopter can provide suppressing fire while the other extracts the soldiers. *U.S. Air Force*

hoist. (If the pilot is injured, one of the two pararescue-men aboard the helicopter can fast-rope to the ground to provide assistance.) The rescue hoist has a 200-foot-long cable with a 600-pound lift capability. It can recover a Stokes litter patient or up to three people simultaneously on a forest penetrator, which resembles an anchor in shape.

All rescue missions begin with extensive planning. Maps are carefully reviewed to identify obstacles, hazardous terrain, and enemy threats, to permit plotting a safe and expedient air route. Often, planners start from the objective and work backward, taking advantage of terrain masking and avoiding enemy radar facilities, populated areas, and air-defense units. When possible, they also avoid having the helicopter cross ridge lines and flat, open terrain. Ingress and egress routes are intentionally different so the Pave Hawk does not fly over threats that may have been alerted during the ingress.

Additionally, using computer data-handling systems such as Constant Source and Sentinel Byte, planners overlay intelligence data on maps to develop so-called spider routes that show the enemy's radar coverage based on terrain, altitude, and the Pave Hawk's radar cross section. Computer programs can also predict the performance of the aircrew's night-vision goggles (NVG) and the helicopter's FLIR system,

Two pararescue jumpers (PJs) prepare to board an HH-60H Pave Hawk using its hoist cable. PJs are highly trained medical technicians whose role is to provide rescue services under combat conditions. They are part of the air force's 720th Special Tactics Group, which is equivalent to the Army's Green Berets and the Navy's SEAL Teams. PJs reportedly participated in the rescue of injured prisoner of war PFC Jessica Lynch from Saddam Hospital in An Nasiriya, Iraq, during Operation Iraqi Freedom. *U.S. Air Force*

An HH-60G Pave Hawk crew chief (*left*) and flight engineer (*right*) discuss last-minute details before flying a mission in support of Operation Northern Watch, the ongoing operation to keep Iraqi military aircraft from flying into northern Iraq after the 1991 Gulf War. *U.S. Air Force*

nation, cultural lighting), turning the world into different shades of green. The difference between the two types of goggles is that the AVS-7 includes a built-in Heads-Up Display, which overlays critical flight information (e.g., airspeed, attitude, torque, compass heading) on the goggle imagery. This means the pilot can pay more attention to flying instead of having to look down at the instrument panel.

Regardless of which NVG is used, the pilot and aircrew have to get used to everything they see as being green. Objects that do not reflect light well, such as pine forests (which reflect only 11 to 13 percent of the ambient light), appear dark green when viewed through night-vision goggles. By contrast, objects that reflect light well, such as snow (which reflects 85 percent of the ambient light), appear lime green. Following this logic, when viewed from the air, lakes and rivers are black, and leafy trees are mint green.

One problem with night-vision goggles is that they wash out when the lighting becomes bright, which makes them useless to the aircrew. This can happen when flying directly into a low-angle moon or setting sun. Muzzle blast from the Pave Hawk's machine guns can also cause washout if they are fired directly forward. Heavy rainstorms, bright spotlights, and dust or snow kicked up when the helicopter lands or hovers also degrade the performance of night-vision goggles.

Lack of depth perception is another common problem associated with NVGs. For example, when flying over flat terrain or large bodies of water, it can be difficult for the pilot to judge the helicopter's altitude. It is easy to begin a slow descent and not realize it until it is too late. Hence, pilots often use the Pave Hawk's Voice Altitude Warning System to avoid this.

based on environmental and tactical information. Once a route has been selected, a final route threat analysis is done, to ensure that nothing has been overlooked.

Since darkness increases the chance of surprise and decreases the chance of the Pave Hawk's being detected and fired upon, most rescues take place at night. Using night-vision goggles and FLIR, the Pave Hawk crew flies just above the tree line, following the contours of the earth toward the downed pilot's location.

Pilots wear either the AVS-6 or the AVS-7 helmet-mounted night-vision goggles. Both amplify available light sources (e.g., starlight, moon, background illumi-

An HH-60G Pave Hawk from the 66th Expeditionary Rescue Squadron takes off from a forward-deployed base in Afghanistan in support of Operation Enduring Freedom in April 2002. In this photo, you can see the helicopter's refueling probe, the FLIR and all-weather radar on the nose, and, of course, the six-barreled minigun. The crew of five includes the pilot, copilot, flight engineer, and two pararescuemen, who also assist with the weapons. *U.S. Air Force*

While night-vision goggles perform best when the helicopter is flying low and slow, electric power lines, unlighted towers, poles, antennas, dead trees, and all types of wires are still difficult to see. This means the aircrew always has to be alert, which can be tiring.

To narrow down the location of a downed pilot, the Pave Hawk is equipped with the ARS-6 Personnel Locator.

It sends out an interrogation burst signal that looks for the PRC-112 radio used by the downed pilot. (The pilot's unique locator code is programmed into the ARS-6.) If the frequency and ID code of the ARS-6 are correct, the pilot's radio sends back a reply, which provides range and steering information to the Pave Hawk. Within seconds, the helicopter is directly over the survivor, ready for rescue.

Loadmasters aboard a C-17 Globemaster III cargo plane from the 17th Expeditionary Airlift Squadron prepare to unload a UH-60L Black Hawk helicopter. All H-60 helicopters have folding rotor blades, which enables them to be placed aboard aircraft for deployment anywhere in the world. It takes only a few hours to reassemble the helicopters after their arrival. *U.S. Air Force*

Occasionally, America's signals intelligence (SIGINT) systems can be used to identify and pinpoint a downed pilot's search-and-rescue beacon. Historically, these systems are used to gather intelligence on the enemy, but they can be called upon to support a rescue operation. Examples of SIGINT systems include high-flying aircraft such as the U-2 and RC-135, and spy satellites such as Magnum and White Cloud. The ability of any of these to actually assist depends on several variables, including the duration of the signal, angle of transmission to the SIGINT system, and strength of the signal beacon.

When conducting a combat search-and-rescue mission, the HH-60G Pave Hawk always flies with another helicopter—either another Pave Hawk or an MH-53J Pave Low—for two reasons. First, if one helicopter is shot down, the other can rescue the crew. Second, while the Pave Hawk is recovering the downed pilot or Special Operations Force (SOF) personnel, the other can provide suppressive machine-gun fire, keeping the enemy at bay.

Since most rescue missions take place at night, a Pave Hawk cannot use normal white lights to find downed personnel. Instead, the aircrew—which is still wearing

The loadmaster aboard an HC-130 Combat Talon special operations aircraft keeps a close eye on the Pave Hawk helicopter as it refuels, looking for signs of potential problems. The Combat Talon is streaming a low-speed refueling drogue, which is used by rotary aircraft. It has an outside diameter of about 46 inches and an inside diameter of about 27 inches. Both the Combat Talon and the Pave Hawk must be flying at the exact same speed and in the same direction to successfully accomplish the refueling mission. *U.S. Air Force*

This photograph, taken from the left-side cargo door facing forward, shows the gunner strapped into position aboard a Pave Hawk to provide suppressive fire if necessary. The gun is actually a six-barreled minigun with a selectable firing rate of 2,000 or 4,000 rounds per minute. On missions, the Pave Hawk has 8,000 rounds of ammunition for each minigun it carries. The tube attached to the weapon directs spent cartridges down and away from the helicopter, so they don't strike the tail rotor or bounce around inside the fuselage, hitting the crew. *U.S. Air Force*

The title of this photograph could be "Speak softly and carry a big gun." In 2002, Airman Vanessa Dobos became the first woman aerial gunner in the U.S. Air Force. As a gunner and member of a combat search-and-rescue crew on a Pave Hawk, she provides suppressive fire while soldiers or downed aviators are extracted from enemy territory. The weapon shown in this photograph is a six-barreled minigun that can fire 4,000 rounds per minute. *U.S. Air Force*

red chemstick is attached to the bottom of each of the three paddles on the forest penetrator.

Typically, a pararescueman (PJ, or pararescue jumper) deploys from the Pave Hawk to assist the downed aviator, especially if the aviator is injured or unconscious. When hoisting the pilot aboard, the helicopter aircrew must take immediate action to prevent the cable from rotating or swinging uncontrollably. Otherwise, the aviator(s) and PJ could be thrown off the hoist—possibly to their deaths.

night-vision goggles—relies on infrared (IR) floodlights, laser pointers, and chemlights to illuminate the objective area. Crew members often use handheld laser pointers to rope the downed pilot or landing zone with a circling motion, making it easier for the Pave Hawk pilot to see where he has to hover or land for recovery. The IR floodlight can then be used, if needed, to illuminate that area. Otherwise, bundles of infrared chemsticks are dropped to the ground to help define the landing zone.

Colored chemsticks are used to help the downed pilot—who is not wearing NVGs—find the hoist, litter, or rope ladder for extraction. For instance, when a rope ladder is used, the Pave Hawk aircrew affixes a red chemstick on each side of the ladder at the first and fifth rungs from the bottom. When the hoist is used, a

MH-60G Specifications

Crew: Four—two officers (pilots) and two enlisted (flight engineer and aerial gunner, or two flight engineers, depending on mission profile)

Length: 64 feet, 9 inches

Height: 16 feet, 9 inches

Rotor diameter: 53 feet, 9 inches

Maximum takeoff weight: 22,500 pounds

Engines: Two General Electric T700-G-700 or T700-FE-701C engines

Speed: 184 mph cruise (220 mph maximum)

Range: 580 statute miles (unlimited with aerial refueling)

Ceiling: 19,000 feet

Active force inventory: 10

Weapons: Two 7.62mm miniguns mounted in the cabin windows, plus two .50-caliber machine guns mounted in the cabin doors. The Pave Hawk can also be equipped with external munitions, depending on mission requirements.

Unit cost: $10.1 million (1992 dollars)

Covert Missions

The army's Green Berets, Delta Force, and Rangers are responsible for conducting unconventional warfare, which encompasses guerrilla warfare, sabotage, intelligence, evasion and escape, and other covert missions. The air force supports the army by using its MH-60G Pave Hawk to help insert, extract, and resupply those soldiers as well as participate in missions involving surveillance, fire support, and psychological warfare. The MH-60G helicopters, once operated by the air force's Special Operations Command, are now blended with its Air Combat Command.

For all intents and purposes, the MH-60G has all the features of an HH-60G but has also been uniquely modified by the air force for long-range, low-altitude missions over land and water. While many of these alterations are classified, it is generally known that the MH-60G Pave Hawk has greater ballistic protection from enemy weapons fire, longer mission range and endurance, improved infrared countermeasures, and more sophisticated navigation and communication systems. It is also equipped with an over-the-horizon

A Pave Hawk gunner confirms checklist operations of the GAU-2 minigun before heading out for a night-combat search-and-rescue training mission. When firing the weapon at night, the gunner must make certain not to aim forward of the helicopter since the bright muzzle flash will wash out the pilot's and copilot's night-vision goggles, effectively blinding them. To help the gunner better aim his minigun, night-vision-goggle-compatible tracer rounds are often inserted every sixth bullet in the ammo belt. *U.S. Air Force*

Right: A pararescue jumper fast-ropes into the Kuwaiti desert from an HH-60G Pave Hawk helicopter. The rope is about 1-1/2 inches in diameter and serves as a quasi fireman's pole. The PJ essentially free-falls to the ground, using glove friction to control his descent. *U.S. Air Force*

Pararescue jumpers from the 129th Rescue Wing climb up a rope ladder from the cold waters surrounding the Golden Gate Bridge to their HH-60G Pave Hawk helicopter. This unique water-retrieval method requires that the PJs be 25 to 30 feet apart in the water while the helicopter moves forward in a level hover at 5 mph. The safetyman aboard the Pave Hawk ensures that at least two rungs of the ladder are in the water, so the PJ can loop an arm over a rung and then climb up. The pilot must fly with extreme care as he deals with gusting winds, sea spray, sun glare, and unexpectedly large sea swells. *U.S. Air Force*

miniguns are two .50-caliber machine guns mounted in the helicopter's doorways.

Should a combat mission warrant it, an MH-60G Pave Hawk can be equipped with the External Stores Support System so it can carry more powerful weapons, such as 20mm cannons and 70mm aerial rockets. Warheads for the popular rockets include high-explosive submunitions, shaped charges to be used against armored targets, flechettes to be used against enemy soldiers, illumination rounds to provide light at night, and an electronic-warfare round to provide jamming, decoy, or countermeasure avoidance.

Since surprise is vital for a special-operations mission to be successful, most take place at night or in adverse weather conditions. Hence the Pave Hawk

An HH-60G Pave Hawk recovers a pararescue jumper using a so-called forest penetrator during a search-and-rescue training exercise. The forest penetrator resembles a boat anchor in appearance, but it has fold-down arms the survivor sits on while being hoisted aboard the helicopter. Up to three people (combined 600-pound limit) can be rescued in this manner simultaneously using just one device. *U.S. Air Force*

tactical data receiver capable of receiving near-real-time combat mission information. This allows the helicopter crew to revise its plan based on the most current data.

The MH-60G, equipped with a GAU-2B 7.62mm minigun in each side window, is more heavily armed than its search-and-rescue cousin.

The six-barreled, electrically driven weapon provides devastating firepower, with the aerial gunner selecting a rate of fire of either 2,000 or 4,000 rounds per minute. Supplementing these

A Pave Hawk helicopter hovers over a forest clearing on a foggy autumn morning as an armed combat controller provides security on the ground. The Pave Hawk uses all-weather radar, FLIR, and a slew of navigation systems to help it fly in nearly all weather conditions, day or night. *U.S. Air Force*

flight crew relies heavily on NVGs, FLIR, weather radar, and precision navigation systems to hug the earth while avoiding obstacles and enemy threats.

The helicopter has a retractable in-flight refueling probe, which enables it to be topped off by an airborne refueler such as the HC-130N/P Combat Shadow before initiating the final legs of its mission. Despite this, it generally must rely on internal auxiliary fuel tanks to reach the objective and return. To maximize its range, the Pave Hawk can be equipped with either the single, 117-gallon tank, which offers 3 hours and 20 minutes of aircraft operations, or the dual 185-gallon tanks, which provide 4-1/2 hours of unrefueled operations.

Special-operations forces are inserted in one of three ways: landing, fast-rope, or rappel. By far the fastest method is fastroping, in which a soldier performs a semicontrolled drop to the ground—much like a fireman sliding down a pole, only faster. Using this technique, a Pave Hawk can unload 8 to 10 combat-equipped soldiers in less than 15 seconds. This significantly limits the helicopter's and soldiers' exposure time to enemy forces.

Fast-roping is done from a 50-foot-high or lower hover. When the Pave Hawk is five minutes out from the objective, the soldiers move to the front of the helicopter, and the safetyman—usually the flight engineer—affixes a fast-rope above each doorway. As the helicopter drops into a hover, the pilot flying gives the command "Ropes, Ropes, Ropes," and the fast-ropes are immediately tossed out. Once the safetyman confirms that the ropes are on the ground, he gives the "Go!" command, and the soldiers quickly deploy, one after the other.

To help soldiers during night operations, a green chemstick is taped vertically at the top of the fast-rope,

Members of the 41st Rescue Squadron push an HH-60G Pave Hawk out of a C-5 Galaxy transport aircraft at Hoedspruit Air Force Base in South Africa in March 2000. The Galaxy delivered cargo, personnel, and two Pave Hawks to support Operation Atlas Response, a humanitarian relief mission that provided food and medicine to victims of a severe flood in Mozambique and South Africa. The Pave Hawks assisted in distributing the supplies and rescuing stranded victims. *U.S. Air Force*

The pilot of an HH-60G Pave Hawk uses a map to reference the helicopter's location during a mission to drop off pararescue personnel for jungle survival training in the Philippines. *U.S. Air Force*

so everyone knows where the rope is located. Two red chemsticks are taped at the bottom of the fast-rope and another 10 feet from the bottom. The latter enables the spotter to relay hover directions to the pilot, so that at least 10 feet of rope is always on the ground, despite the helicopter's up-and-down movement.

Rappelling, while requiring more specialized equipment and preparation than fast-roping, is useful when high hovers are necessary, such as above a thickly forested area. Up to three rappel ropes can be affixed to each side of the Pave Hawk, enabling six soldiers to descend simultaneously.

When extracting soldiers, the MH-60G Pave Hawk either lands or relies on a rope ladder. Hoisting is not

feasible in combat situations, because it takes too long to retrieve an entire team.

Should the Pave Hawk come under enemy fire during insertion or extraction—while hovering—the pilot turns the tail toward the fire, to expose the smallest area to the enemy while shielding the cabin and cockpit. If the flight engineer or gunner is able to return fire, the pilot can decide to turn the Pave Hawk to engage the enemy with 7.62mm or .50-caliber machine guns.

During the 1991 Gulf War, MH-60G Pave Hawks provided combat search-and-rescue coverage for coalition air forces in western Iraq, Saudi Arabia, coastal Kuwait, and the Persian Gulf. They also provided emergency

evacuation coverage for Navy SEAL teams penetrating the Kuwaiti coast before the invasion.

During Operation Allied Force, MH-60G Pave Hawks successfully rescued the pilots of an F-117 Nighthawk and an F-16C Fighting Eagle shot down by Serbian missiles. The latter entailed a predawn rescue effort involving a Pave Hawk and two MH-53J Pave Low helicopters. The F-16 pilot, Hammer 34, was just a few seconds away from being captured by Serbian forces when the Pave Hawk—dodging missiles and small-arms fire—swooped in. A combat controller and PJ leapt out and provided covering fire until Hammer 34 was safely aboard the helicopter. Then, with an armed MH-53J on either side, the Pave Hawk sandwich-zoomed for friendly territory, evading spotlights and antiaircraft artillery.

Top: A Pave Hawk helicopter painted in a desert camouflage scheme has just inserted special-operations forces into the water, along with their inflatable boats. This image was taken during the 1991 Gulf War. *Department of Defense*

Special-operations forces—most likely Navy SEALs—prepare to board a Pave Hawk helicopter. Due to the lack of weapons (they are armed only with knives), this is undoubtedly a training mission. This image was taken in the Persian Gulf region in 1990–91. *Department of Defense*

Despite the ocean's vastness, it is anything but empty . . . or safe. More than 600 submarines operated by 42 nations call this environment home, meaning that a warship—especially an aircraft carrier—is always in the crosshairs of enemy periscopes and in the dreams of submariners. To escape detection, submarines routinely use Mother Nature's features to their own advantage.

For instance, to avoid being detected by ships and aircraft, submarines often hide below the ocean's thermocline (a layer of dense, cold water that reflects and refracts sound waves) or deep scatter layer (an underwater zone made up of floating microscopic plants and animal life that scatter acoustic waves). With cunning, patience, and a little luck, a sub skipper can position himself to fire a few tin fish at a ship.

As a result of this underwater threat, an aircraft carrier never puts to sea alone. It is always accompanied by up to a dozen ships that defend the carrier against enemy attack and assist it in waging war. These escorts—mostly cruisers, destroyers, and frigates—fan out across the ocean ahead of and around the aircraft carrier, to establish a submarine exclusion zone. While the radius of this zone varies with the carrier battle group's operating area, one thing is certain: it is aggressively patrolled by Seahawk antisubmarine-warfare helicopters.

SH-60B Specifications

Crew: Three or four—pilot, copilot/tactical systems operator, acoustics systems operator

Length: 64 feet, 10 inches; 41 feet, 6 inches folded

Height: 17 feet, 2 inches

Rotor diameter: 53 feet, 8 inches

Empty weight: 14,872 pounds

Mission gross weight: 21,110 pounds (anti-submarine-warfare role); 19,226 pounds (anti-ship surveillance and targeting role); 21,884 pounds (maximum gross takeoff weight)

Engines: Two General Electric T700-GE-401C turboshaft engines

Dash speed: 161 mph

Endurance: 58-mile radius with a 3-hour loiter; 172-mile radius with a 1-hour loiter

Ceiling: 19,000 feet

Auxiliary fuel: Up to two external tanks

Weapons: Three external store stations for Mk-46/50 torpedoes, AGM-119B Penguin anti-ship missile, and AGM-114 Hellfire air-to-surface and air-to-air missiles

Opposite: An SH-60B Seahawk successfully launches an AGM-119 Penguin anti-ship missile at a target ship during a naval training exercise. The fire-and-forget missile hit a former *Knox*-class frigate just 24 inches above the waterline, its 265-pound high-explosive warhead sinking the ship. The Penguin can travel in excess of 25 miles at Mach 1.2. SH-60 helicopters can also carry the AGM-114 Hellfire laser-guided missile, which is used to shoot down enemy helicopters and slow-moving airplanes and to punch holes in bunkers and surface ships. Interestingly, the SH-60B was designed to carry a nuclear depth charge to sink Soviet submarines but was never wired to carry out that mission. The B-57 nuclear depth bomb had a 5 to 10 kiloton yield. *U.S. Navy*

This image epitomizes the role of the SH-60F Ocean Hawk—protection of the area immediately surrounding the aircraft carrier of a battle group from hostile submarines. The helicopter also serves as plane guard, rescuing downed aviators who crash after taking off or before landing. To protect the helicopter's crew from a dunking at sea, emergency flotation bags are installed in the stub wing fairing on the main landing gear on both sides of the helicopter. The pilot deploys the bags if the Seahawk has to make an emergency landing in the ocean. *U.S. Navy*

At the height of the Cold War in the late 1960s, the U.S. Navy became concerned about advancements in the Soviet Union's standoff weapon systems and the stealth-like capabilities of its submarines. The navy quickly realized it needed to expand the protective bubble around the surface fleet. At the time, the navy was using the large, boat-hulled SH-3 Sea King helicopter to fly antisubmarine (ASW) missions. However, its size did not allow many frigates and destroyers to carry it.

The Chief of Naval Operations requested that the navy investigate the possibility of flying antisubmarine and antiship surveillance missions with a smaller but more capable helicopter that could be deployed throughout the fleet. The result was the 1970 LAMPS

Rescuing someone behind enemy lines is inherently dangerous. Here, two aircrew personnel assigned to the Black Knights of Helicopter Anti-Submarine Squadron Four (HS-4) prepare for a combat search-and-rescue mission aboard the aircraft carrier USS *Abraham Lincoln* (CVN-72). They will conduct the mission on an HH-60H Combat Support Helicopter. *U.S. Navy*

program for a Light Airborne Multi-Purpose System. Packed with state-of-the-art sensors, this helicopter would significantly extend the range of a warship's radar capabilities by as much as 100 miles, to see well beyond the horizon and attack enemy submarines and missile-equipped surface ships.

The LAMPS role was initially fulfilled by installing sensors used aboard ships on the Kaman SH-2 Seasprite helicopter, which the navy already had in its inventory.

When that proved successful, the navy upgraded the system to a more advanced LAMPS Mk II configuration. But that ended up being too much for the Seasprite to handle, so the navy canceled the program and wrote new requirements for a LAMPS Mk III version.

In a surprising move, the prime contract was awarded to IBM and not to an aircraft company, reflecting the overriding importance of the avionics systems to the navy. So, while IBM moved ahead to develop the flight control, navigation, mission-search, and weapon-delivery systems, the navy busied itself in finding a helicopter platform to put it all on.

As luck would have it, the army was evaluating helicopters for its UTTAS program at the time. They had narrowed the search down to the Boeing Vertol YUH-61A and the Sikorsky YUH-60A. The navy, feeling that both aircraft appeared suitable for its LAMPS Mk III mission, began its own evaluation. In late 1976, the army selected the Sikorsky helicopter.

This influenced the navy's decision, and not because of the 83 percent commonality between the army and navy helicopters, which promised a significant reduction in unit price. In late summer 1977, the navy went with the Sikorsky contender, designating it the SH-60B Seahawk. At the same time, General Electric was given a contract to further develop its turboshaft engine, which would power the Seahawk, to provide increased power and improved resistance to saltwater corrosion.

Navy SEALs fastrope aboard a Mk V patrol craft, operated by Special Boat Squadrons to covertly insert and extract special-operations forces in times of war. The Mk V is an amazingly powerful and fast boat, reaching speeds of 50 mph. *U.S. Navy*

As is evident, the innards of an SH-60 are close and cozy. There is adequate room to lie down, but not to stand. Here, navy SEALs relax before participating in a training exercise, which explains the "bone dome" helmet and swim fins they are wearing. *U.S. Navy*

After years of testing and design modifications, the SH-60B Seahawk entered navy service in January 1983. Light Helicopter Anti-Submarine Squadron 41 (HSL-41), at Naval Air Station North Island, became the first Seahawk squadron. It began providing detachments of the ASW helicopters for deployment aboard so-called "small boys"—*Ticonderoga*-class cruisers, *Spruance*-class destroyers, and *Oliver Hazard Perry*–class frigates. Each warship in these classes carries two SH-60B Seahawks.

Although the basic Seahawk helicopter resembles its UH-60A Black Hawk cousin, it features several important differences. For instance, unlike the army helicopter, the Seahawk has a rotor brake, to prevent the rotor from spinning when the helo is parked aboard a ship. This is important, because a ship steaming at sea always has enough air moving over it to turn the rotor. As for the rotor blades themselves, they are not folded manually but by electric power.

Additionally, the Seahawk's tailwheel has been moved forward, under the fuselage, to help ensure that it does not slip over the edge of a ship's deck when the helicopter is landing. If it did, the helo could possibly do a backflip into the ocean.

Since space is always at a premium aboard ships, the entire tail pylon of the helicopter is hinged, so it

An SH-60F "Ocean Hawk" helicopter sits on the flight deck of the USS *John F. Kennedy* (CV-67), armed with a 7.62mm machine gun and four laser-guided AGM-114 Hellfire air-to-ground missiles. If necessary, the helicopter can be outfitted with other weapons, such as .50-caliber machine guns and 70mm aerial rockets. *U.S. Navy*

can be unlocked and folded flat against the tailboom. This decreases the Seahawk's length by about 24 feet.

Another difference between the Black Hawk and the Seahawk is that the Seahawk has Recovery Assist, Secure and Traverse (RAST) to help it land on the pitching deck of a ship. RAST is a cable-and-winch system that connects to the underside of a Seahawk hovering over the deck. The cable gives the pilot 4,000 pounds of hauldown force, to center and safely pull the

helicopter onto the deck. After this, another part of the RAST mechanism tows the helicopter into the ship's hangar. Using this device, a Seahawk can land in Sea State 5 conditions—12-foot waves and 38 mph winds. Hence, the SH-60B Seahawk can perform its ASW role in nearly any type of weather.

Antisubmarine warfare is indeed the primary role of the Seahawk, although the helicopter can also be used for search-and-rescue, vertical replenishment, medical evacuation, and anti-surface-warfare operations. To achieve its ASW mission, the helicopter uses its various sensors—search radar, magnetic anomaly detector, electronic support measures, sonobuoys, and dipping sonar—to detect, classify, and attack hostile submarines.

The SH-60B Seahawk deploys from its parent ship when the warship's powerful hull-mounted sonar or towed passive-sonar array detects a submarine. The helicopter dashes out to the target area and strategically drops a number of sonobuoys into the ocean to encircle the submarine. A sonobuoy is a 3-foot-long, tube-shaped device that detects a sub either actively (reflected acoustical pulse) or passively (propeller cavitation, machinery or hydrodynamic sounds). The navy uses a number of different sonobuoys.

On the Seahawk, the sonobuoys are ejected from a 25-tube launcher located on the left side of the fuselage, behind the cabin door. When the buoy hits the water, its battery is activated, the transmission antenna extends, and the hydrophone is lowered to a predetermined depth (60–1,500 feet) by cable. Underwater sounds detected by the hydrophone are transmitted to the helicopter, where they are passed back to the ship via a secure, high-speed digital radio signal. Staff in the ship's Combat Information Center can not only analyze the data in real time but also control many of the helicopter's LAMPS III systems remotely, if necessary.

If the sonobuoys are not used—generally in situations where the helicopter does not want to tip its presence to the submarine's crew—the Seahawk can trail a retractable, yellow-and-red

During an antisubmarine training exercise, an Acoustic Systems Operator in the cabin of a Seahawk strategically dispenses sonobuoys into the ocean. The sonobuoys' pattern enables the helicopter to detect and hunt down enemy submarines in the area. *U.S. Navy*

A technician loads sonobuoys into the horizontal launching dispenser on an SH-60B Seahawk. The navy uses a wide variety of these expendable, passive and active acoustic sensors to detect submerged submarines. The sonobuoy being loaded in this photo is the SSQ-53 DIFAR (Directional low-Frequency Acquisition and Ranging), a passive directional sensor that can be deployed at depths of 100, 400, or 1,000 feet, listening for telltale sounds in the 10 hertz to 2.4 kilohertz frequency range. *U.S. Navy*

has a range of about 11,000 yards and can dive to more than 1,200 feet. Its warhead consists of 95 pounds of PBXN-103 high explosive.

SH 60F Specifications

Crew: Four—pilot, copilot, tactical systems operator, acoustics systems operator
Length: 64 feet, 10 inches; 40 feet, 11 inches folded
Height: 17 feet
Rotor diameter: 53 feet, 8 inches
Mission gross weight: 21,800 pounds
Engines: Two General Electric T700-GE-401C turboshaft engines
Dash speed: 153 mph
Auxiliary fuel: One internal auxiliary tank and one external auxiliary tank
Endurance: 4.2 hours, depending on conditions
Weapons: M60D 7.62mm machine guns and three external store stations for Mk-50 torpe does, AGM-119B Penguin air-to-surface anti-ship missile, or AGM-114 Hellfire air-to-ground anti-armor missiles. For most ASW missions, the CV Helo deploys with two Mk-50 torpedoes.

magnetic anomaly detector (also known as a bird) behind it. The sensor picks up disturbances of the earth's magnetic field as a submarine—which is large and mostly metal—passes through it. The bird is deployed from a housing on the Seahawk's right rear side.

Once the submarine's position has been pinpointed, the Seahawk drops a high-speed, deep-diving Mk-46 Lightweight Torpedo. After entering the water, the torpedo executes a helical search pattern until it detects the submarine with its acoustic sensor. It then attacks at a speed of about 50 mph. If it misses, it automatically reacquires the sub and continues with the attack. The Mk-46 reportedly

CV Helo

The SH-60B Seahawk and its parent ship are responsible for searching a 65- to 80-square-mile sector of ocean for submarines, far in advance of the carrier battle group to which it belongs. By contrast, the SH-60F helicopter is embarked on the aircraft carrier itself to provide quick-reaction ASW protection for the inner zone of the battle group, just in case a submarine sneaks past the outer defenses.

Known officially as the CV Helo (CV is the navy's designation for an aircraft carrier), the SH-60F is also informally known as Ocean Hawk. This is to distinguish it from its cousin, the Seahawk, although the CV Helo looks distinctly different. For one thing, it does not have the large, cylindrical search radar beneath its chin. Also, the MAD bird on the right rear is missing, as is the 5-by-5 sonobuoy launch-tube matrix on the left side. Nor does the CV Helo have a RAST system, because landing on an aircraft carrier's flight deck is easier than landing on a "small boy," even in bad weather.

The true difference between a Seahawk and the CV Helo—both of which are LAMPS Mk III helicopters—is in how the CV Helo hunts down a submarine. As one can imagine, the ocean surrounding an aircraft carrier within a 50-mile radius is extremely noisy, due to the turning propellers of not only the aircraft carrier but also of nearby ships, such as replenishment vessels and the guided-missile cruiser or destroyer playing the Red Crown air-combat coordinator role. Hence, it is impossible to hear a submarine using passive, underwater-listening sensors.

One solution to this problem is active sonar—where a strong acoustic wave is sent out that returns a distinct "ping!" if the wave bounces off an object. This is the technology the CV Helo mainly uses to locate submarines. From the belly of the helicopter, a tethered AQS-113F dipping sonar is lowered by cable into the ocean while the pilot uses a radar altimeter and the automatic flight-control system to maintain a 50-foot hover. The sonar, which operates at depths up to 1,450 feet, is sensitive enough to detect a submarine

A crew member of Helicopter Anti-Submarine Squadron Four (HS-4) Black Knights rushes to the aid of a downed aviator during a training exercise. Most combat search-and-rescue missions take place under cover of darkness—using night-vision equipment—to thwart detection by enemy forces. Two helicopters, manned by two pilots and three crew members each, are used for training and, if called upon, for an actual mission. *U.S. Navy*

11 miles away while determining its range, range rate, and bearing. If necessary, the helicopter can "jump dip" to quickly reposition the sonar to track an evasive sub.

In some cases, such as when encircling a submarine with listening devices, the CV Helo may wish to deploy active/passive sonobuoys. In these situations, the expendable sonobuoys are ejected downward from a launcher mounted in the floor of the helicopter. As many as six sonobuoys can be deployed before the launcher requires reloading by the Tactical Systems Operator (TSO) from a storage carousel mounted inside the fuselage.

While the Acoustic Systems Operator (ASO) is analyzing the data streaming into his console from either the dipping sonar or sonobuoys, the TSO—who sits beside him in the cabin—concentrates on

"Splish splash, we're taking a bath." Actually, two rescue swimmers hone their skills by jumping from an SH-60B Seahawk into the water. While the SH-60B is primarily an anti-submarine-warfare helicopter operating from cruisers, destroyers, and frigates, it also plays a search-and-rescue role in recovering downed aviators. *U.S. Navy*

getting an overall view of the situation by monitoring the radar, acoustics, electronic support measures, and so on being linked to him from his own helicopter and other ships and SH-60B Seahawks participating in the hunt. Running the operation and figuring out when and where to drop sonobuoys or to reposition other helicopters is a demanding job. In the end, if he fails at his task, the sub could either slink away or, worse, successfully launch a torpedo at the aircraft carrier.

Navy SEALs practice a Helicopter Visit, Board, Search, and Seizure (HVBSS). Quickly disembarking from the HH-60H Combat Support Helicopter by fastrope, they spread out and assume a tactical formation to take control of the ship. The second helicopter in the background is in position to provide suppressing fire and to radio information to the SEALs about what the ship's crew is doing. *U.S. Navy*

As with the SH-60B Seahawk, all LAMPS III acoustics data from the CV Helo is shared with the battle group through the Anti-Submarine Classification and Analysis Center (ASCAC), which is installed aboard *Nimitz*-class aircraft carriers. ASCAC permits real-time sharing of information between the carrier, its ASW aircraft, and task force escorts.

When the submarine's location is known, the CV Helo drops a Mk. 50 Advanced Lightweight Torpedo. Known as the Barracuda, this torpedo is faster than the Mk. 46, has greater endurance, and can dive deeper. It also has better terminal homing, a programmable digital computer, and more destructive power. The 750-pound Barracuda is powered by a unique, stored-chemical-energy propulsion system that provides full power at all depths and can furnish multi-speed settings as required by the situation at hand. The Mk. 50 has a speed in excess of 58 miles per hour and a maximum diving depth of about 1,950 feet. Its 100-pound high-explosive, shaped charge can penetrate the toughest submarine hulls, including

An Acoustic Systems Operator (ASO) sits at his console aboard an SH-60F Ocean Hawk, monitoring every sound detected by the dipping sonar (or submerged sonobuoys). The sounds are also relayed via a secure, high-speed digital signal to the helicopter's parent ship, which uses the data to wage undersea warfare. *U.S. Navy*

titanium.

While the main role of the CV Helo is to investigate potential submarine contacts near the aircraft carrier, it also assumes all the roles of its SH-60B Seahawk sister (i.e., fleet support operations, logistics, medical evacuation, search-and-rescue) *plus* the role of plane guard. This means it flies in formation with the aircraft carrier—astern and to one side, where it can see everything—

while aircraft take off and land on the carrier. This is in case an F/A-18 Hornet, EA-6B Prowler, E-2C Hawkeye, or other plane crashes into the ocean, requiring rescue of the aviators with the helicopter's external hoist. Both the ASO and TSO are trained in rescue procedures.

The SH-60F CV Helo began delivery with the navy in 1988. The first fleet squadron to receive the SH-60F was Helicopter Anti-Submarine Squadron 2 (HS-2), the

HH-60H Specifications

Crew: Three—pilot, copilot, crew chief/gunner

Length: 64 feet, 10 inches; 40 feet, 11 inches folded

Height: 17 feet

Rotor diameter: 53 feet, 8 inches

Engines: Two General Electric T700-GE-401C turboshaft engines

Cruise speed: 170 mph at sea level

Range: 230–90-mile radius with 30-minute loiter; maximum 470-mile range

Auxiliary fuel: Two 120-gallon external auxiliary tanks

Aircraft survivability systems: Infrared countermeasures; two chaff and flare dispensers; radar warning receiver; emergency locator; hover infrared suppressor system

Weapons: M60D 7.62mm machine guns; AGM-114 Hellfire air-to-ground anti-armor-missile–capable; GAU-2 Gatling gun–capable; 70mm Hydra rocket launcher–capable

A Navy SEAL from SEAL Team 8 covers his squad from a Seahawk helicopter as they conduct a "takedown" training exercise aboard the USS *LaSalle* (AGF-3). The *LaSalle* serves as the flagship for the commander of the Sixth Fleet and is outfitted with extensive command, control, communications, and intelligence equipment. *U.S. Navy*

Golden Falcons, in March 1990.

Combat Support Helicopter

If you strip an SH-60F of all its ASW gear and add a door on the left side, you are left with something that resembles the HH-60H helicopter, which is used by the navy to insert, extract, and resupply its SEAL teams. The helicopter is flown by Reserve Helicopter Combat Support Squadrons (Special) HCS-4 Red Wolves (NAS Norfolk, Virginia) and HCS-5 Firehawks (NAS Point Magu, California), both of which were established in 1989 to provide support to naval special-warfare units.

The HH-60H, which is nicknamed Warhawk by some in the special-operations community, can carry up to eight SEALs and their equipment. The SEALs are inserted by fastrope, paradrop, or rappel. A commonly used water-insertion tactic is for the Warhawk to hover 10 feet above the ocean and release an inflatable boat fastened to the underside of the fuselage. The SEALs then jump from the helicopter's side into the water to man the boat and continue the operation. (The helo moves forward slowly during this process, to prevent the SEALs from landing atop one another.) Using this technique, it takes only about 10 seconds for the helo to unload and go. The flight crews of HCS-4 and HCS-5 are trained in low-altitude night-flight operations using night-vision devices.

For self-protection, the Warhawk is armed with two

An SH-60 helicopter deploys flares as a countermeasure to thwart an incoming heat-seeking missile. The missile's guidance system tracks the hot-burning flares instead of the helicopter. All Seahawk helos are outfitted with a number of protective measures to avoid being shot down, including infrared absorbing paint, an infrared suppression system on the engines, an active infrared jammer, and, of course, flares. *U.S. Navy*

7.62mm machine guns—one on either side of the cabin—with 4,000 rounds of ammunition each. When necessary, the helo can be outfitted with more powerful weapons, such as the laser-guided Hellfire anti-armor missile and the unguided 70mm aerial rocket. Furthermore, the machine guns can be replaced by either six-barreled 7.62mm miniguns or three-barreled .50-caliber miniguns.

The secondary role of the HH-60H is combat search-and-rescue. Regardless of how skilled a pilot is, the enemy occasionally gets off a lucky shot. When he does, the aviators of the downed aircraft are always happy to see a "Rescue Hawk" come dancing over the trees or ocean waves. Each Helicopter Anti-Submarine Squadron

The helicopter offers an ideal way of getting mail, food, supplies, and men to a submarine. If a ship were used, it would be dangerous to climb the sub's hull carrying cargo while the two vessels are tossed about by the sea. In this photo, it appears that navy SEALs are fastroping aboard a submarine. (A hoist would have been used for others.) Many naval operations rely on using subs to insert SEALs on covert missions. *U.S. Navy*

(HS), which is assigned to an aircraft carrier air wing and flies the SH-60B and SH-60F Seahawk variants, has two HH-60H helicopters for search-and-rescue missions.

Since the navy nearly always operates at sea, most rescues take place over water (although, admittedly, many SEAL missions do take place ashore). Searching for someone in the vastness of the ocean is difficult. First, only the pilot's head and upper chest are visible above the water. Second, ocean waves can be 6 feet

high on a good day—and 20 feet on a bad day—effectively hiding the pilot from view. With a Rescue Hawk pilot flying 500 feet above the surface, it's almost impossible to see an aviator, even if he's waving his arms.

That's why the HH-60H is equipped with a special locator system that homes in on the frequency of the survival radio carried by the downed pilot. As the helicopter approaches, it drops to 100 feet and makes

An excellent view of an airborne SH-60B Seahawk helicopter, complete with a Mk. 46 lightweight torpedo. Toward the rear of the fuselage can be seen the colorful red-and-yellow magnetic anomaly detector (MAD), trailed behind the helicopter to detect a submerged submarine by fluctuations in the earth's magnetic field. Once the sub is found, the high-speed, deep-diving torpedo is dropped.
Richard Zellner/Sikorsky Aircraft

an oval, racetrack-shaped observation pass, deploying green sea-dye markers or colored smoke near the survivor, to mark his location. Rescue efforts are done with the helicopter orienting itself into the wind, to ensure adequate lift while hovering.

If the survivor is injured, unconscious, tangled in his parachute, or unable to get into a rescue device, the helicopter descends to 50 feet and lowers a

Opposite: An SH-60B Seahawk lands aboard a small boy using RAST (Recovery Assist, Secure and Traverse). The cable, once hooked to the helicopter, provides 4,000 pounds of downhaul. This centers and drags the helicopter onto the ship's landing deck, even if the ship is pitching and rolling. The large, round object beneath the chin of the helicopter houses the rotating antenna of the powerful APS-124 Search Radar. *U.S. Navy*

An Aviation Electronics Technician guides the hoist wire at the door of an SH-60F CV Helo while two rescue swimmers are lifted from the ocean during a training session. The horse collar is just one of several ways in which a helicopter can rescue a downed aviator. Other methods include the rescue net, ladder, forest penetrator, and Stokes litter basket. The decision as to which one is used depends on combat circumstances and whether the survivor is injured and/or conscious. *U.S. Navy*

rescue swimmer 10 to 30 yards downwind of the survivor. (In dire circumstances, such as when the survivor is drowning, the helo hovers at 10 feet, and the rescue swimmer jumps into the water.) The swimmer, who wears an anti-exposure suit in waters cooler than 60 degrees to avoid hypothermia, prepares the survivor to be lifted aboard the helicopter using a hoist and sling (also known as a horse collar), Stokes litter, or rescue net. The rescue net is used to scoop the survivor from the ocean and is particularly effective when rescuing someone from frigid waters who is unable to move his limbs as a result of hypothermia.

During the recovery effort, the Rescue Hawk pilot must avoid watching the pickup, since he might become spatially disoriented. This is especially true when the sea is flat, because depth perception is adversely affected. Additionally, there is a tendency for the helicopter to drift backward while hovering over water. This can result in loss of lift, causing the helicopter to descend. If corrective action is not taken, it could crash.

For combat search-and-rescue missions at night, when strobes and flares cannot be used, the flight crew wears night-vision goggles. As the Rescue Hawk makes its observation pass at 50 knots, the pilot defines the extraction zone by ordering the left and right scanners (usually the crew chief and rescue swimmer) to drop infrared or red chemlites into the ocean at his command. The first to be dropped is a chemlite star, which is a bundle of five chemlites tied together to resemble a star pattern in the water. It indicates the beginning of the zone.

One second after entering this zone, the pilot makes three "Throw!" calls about 2 seconds apart. At each

The original *Arleigh Burke*–class destroyers were not designed with helicopter hangars, since the SH-60B Seahawks were initially kept aboard frigates, cruisers, and *Spruance*-class destroyers. But with those ships aging and the *Burkes* playing a greater multi-mission role, it was decided—beginning with USS *Oscar Austin* (DDG-79) in 2000, as shown in this photo—to stretch the length of the destroyers by 6 feet and add a hangar for one ASW Seahawk and one armed attack helicopter. When a helicopter lands aboard this ship, it approaches from the right rear, taking directions from the flight-control booth mounted between the two hangars. RAST is used to pull the helo onto the pitching deck and then drag it into the hangar. *Bath Iron Works*

An SH-60F CV Helo from Helicopter Anti-Submarine Squadron 2 (HS-2) Golden Falcons lowers its AQS-113 active/passive dipping sonar into the ocean to search for hiding submarines. The sonar, which operates at depths up to 1,450 feet, is designed to function in the noisy waters of an aircraft carrier battle group's inner zone. *Sikorsky Aircraft*

Inside the hangar aboard the guided-missile destroyer USS *Roosevelt* (DDG-80) where RAST (*floor track*) is being used to move an SH-60B helicopter from the flight deck. The two white boxes on either side of the helicopter's nose are part of the ALQ-142 passive electronic support measure (ESM) system. It allows the Seahawk to detect hostile enemy radar and radio emissions while remaining silent itself. Two additional boxes located aft of the fuselage give the helicopter 360-degree coverage. The data collected can be used for intelligence and to assist in detecting and targeting enemy ships. *Bath Iron Works*

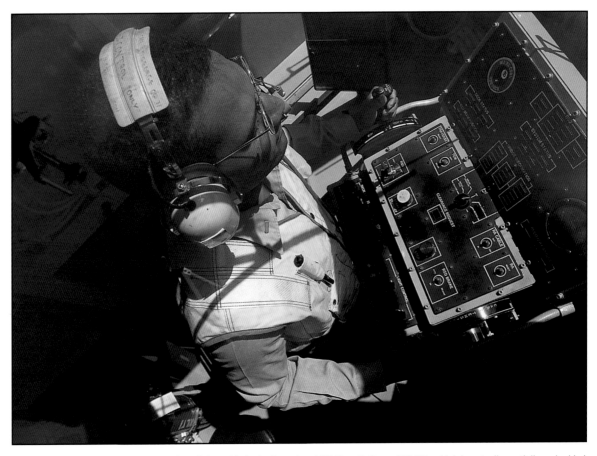

A peek inside the flight-control booth aboard the guided-missile cruiser USS *Cape St. George* (CG-71), which is actually partially embedded in a corner of the ship's helicopter flight deck. The console in front of this sailor controls the RAST (Recovery Assist, Secure and Traverse) system, which helps SH-60 helicopters land safely in rough seas. You can see the Recovery Assist (RA) information on the right-hand side. *S. F. Tomajczyk*

command, the scanners throw a group of three chemlites as hard as possible out either side of the helicopter's cabin. These define the left and right sides of the extraction zone, which is clearly visible using night-vision goggles.

The helicopter then makes a slow, final approach, entering the zone while descending to 10 feet above the water and moving forward at 10 knots. As with a daylight rescue, the rescue swimmer jumps out when he is 10 to 30 yards from the survivor and gives a thumbs-up signal after hitting the water to indicate he is okay and has not sustained any injuries. (In rough seas, the helicopter makes a higher approach and lowers the rescue swimmer by hoist.) When the rescue swimmer is finally ready for pickup, he twirls a red chemlite on a 2-foot string over his head. The hoist operator then reels him and the survivor aboard the helicopter.

A close-up look at an HH-60H Combat Support Helicopter flown by HS-2 Golden Falcons as it prepares to deploy a navy SEAL squad. An inflatable raft, affixed to the underside of the fuselage (you can see part of it in the bottom left of this photo), is dropped first. Then the SEALs jump about 10 feet into the water, where they retrieve the raft and continue with their mission. While conducting this insertion, the helicopter's gunner provides suppressive fire if necessary. *S. F. Tomajczyk*

From start to finish, a rescue operation typically requires up to an hour on-scene. This is especially true if the downed aviator is seriously injured and the Stokes litter must be used. Of all the extraction methods, the litter is the slowest, since the patient must be carefully strapped into the basket without causing additional injury.

CHAPTER FOUR

BIRDS OF A FEATHER

Most civilians forget that the Coast Guard is part of America's armed services. In times of war, it works under the U.S. Navy to enforce the Maritime Defense Zone, which includes antisubmarine warfare, port security, convoy escort, mine countermeasures, and combat search-and-rescue. In this photograph, Marines from Echo Company, 4th Marine Reconnaissance Battalion, wait in a combat rubber raiding craft for other members of their team to jump from the Jayhawk. This training exercise took place in the frigid waters off Sitka, Alaska. *U.S. Coast Guard*

Jayhawk

HH-60J Specifications

Crew: Four
Rotor Diameter: 54 feet
Height: 17 feet
Overall length: 65 feet
Maximum takeoff gross weight: 21,884 pounds
Useful load: 7,609 pounds (includes crew, fuel, and search-and-rescue (SAR) equipment)
Empty weight: 14,022 pounds
Engines: 2 General Electric T700-401C gas turbines
Fuel capacity: 6,460 pounds
Maximum speed: 180 knots
Range: 700 nautical miles
Endurance: 7 hours at cruising speeds of 135–40 knots
Unit cost: $17 million (1991 dollars)

The motto of the U.S. Coast Guard is *Semper Paratus*—"Always Ready"—and the Jayhawk (HH-60J) helicopter plays a vital role in Coasties fulfilling that motto. In 1991, the Jayhawk replaced the Coast Guard's aging fleet of HH-3F Pelican and CH-3E Sea King helicopters as its medium-range recovery helo. While the primary mission of the Jayhawk is search-and-rescue, it also plays an important role in port security, law enforcement, foreign vessel inspection, homeland defense, maritime patrol, and drug interdiction missions.

The helicopter's technical specifications are similar to the navy's SH-60B/F Seahawk, except that the Jayhawk can be fitted with three external fuel tanks that enable it to fly 300 miles offshore, remain on-scene 45 minutes, hoist six people aboard, and return safely to base. (The Jayhawk has a 590-gallon internal fuel capacity and can be externally equipped with two 120-gallon and one 80-gallon pylon fuel tanks.)

While the HH-60J is equipped with navigation systems to help it reach a destination—including the Tactical Air Navigation System, which uses a UHF electronic beacon to continuously provide the helo with a bearing and distance from a known ground-based reference station—the Jayhawk uses the Global Positioning System (GPS) as its long-range navigational aid. Onboard the helicopter, a Collins RCVR-3A radio simultaneously receives information from four of the GPS system's 18 worldwide satellites and instantly converts the data into latitude and longitude fixes, pinpointing the aircraft's position to within three feet.

Other key features of the Jayhawk include a weather/search radar, a radar altimeter (so the pilot knows exactly how high the helicopter is above a target), a secure and jam-resistant Identification Friend or Foe system (to determine if an unidentified aircraft is hostile), cockpit video displays, night-vision-goggle-compatible lighting systems, and dual-redundant mission computers. Triple-redundant electrical and hydraulic systems help ensure the helicopter's survivability, as does a system that automatically controls the Jayhawk's approach, hover, and departure during a rescue effort.

Although the HH-60J Jayhawk can be carried on medium- and high-endurance Coast Guard cutters, other ships in the fleet must still be able to work with the helicopter. Here, the 86-foot cutter *Barracuda* (WPB-87301) practices basket hoists with a Jayhawk. The basket is a Stokes litter, used to transport injured personnel. *U.S. Coast Guard*

The Coast Guard presently operates 42 Jayhawks out of seven air stations. Of these, about 35 of the birds are available at any given time to respond to missions.

Although the Jayhawk is not able to land on water (and thus is normally stationed ashore), it can be carried aboard medium- and high-endurance Coast Guard cutters, such as the U.S.C.G.C *Escanaba* (WMEC-907) and U.S.C.G.C *Boutwell* (WHEC-719).

During Operation Enduring Freedom in 2003, the Coast Guard sent several cutters (and their helos) to the Persian Gulf, where they escorted U.S. vessels, assisted with maritime boarding and interdiction duties, and helped enforce security zones established around ports and anchored U.S. warships, to prevent terrorist attacks. The helicopters constantly patrolled wharves, shore-lines, and the Gulf for approaching boats (such as Zodiac inflatable crafts), trespassers, and suspicious or unauthorized activities.

The Coast Guard provided similar military services during Operation Desert Storm in 1991.

Search-and-Rescue

Search-and-rescue (SAR) is the proverbial meat and potatoes of the Coast Guard. Each year, Coasties save the lives of 3,200 to 4,000 people—which represents a success rate of about 93 percent. (The rate would be higher, but the remaining 7 percent represent people who typically die before or immediately after the Coast Guard is notified, such as in an explosion or sinking.)

Rescue missions are always hazardous, and without a doubt some of the Coast Guard's most hair-raising rescues occur off the coast of Alaska, where high winds, strong ocean currents, and enormous waves batter those who dare to venture out onto the ice-cold Bering Sea. In spite of these dangers, the Alaska fishing fleet heads seaward each January for the famous Opelio Tanner

A Jayhawk helicopter approaches the landing deck of the medium-endurance cutter *Escanaba* (WMEC-907). These multipurpose warships are outfitted with RAST (Recovery Assist, Secure and Traverse), to help the helicopters land in rough seas. In times of war, these cutters would have an SH-60F Seahawk LAMPS III antisubmarine warfare helicopter assigned to them for convoy escort. An expanding hangar would protect the helo from the weather. *U.S. Coast Guard*

crabbing season. And when they do, the Coast Guard knows that despite safety efforts taken (e.g., survival suits, life rafts, Emergency Position Indicating Radio Beacons), many ships and fishermen will not be coming home. In some seasons, as many as 20 ships have sunk and 12 sailors have drowned.

In one such incident, a Jayhawk helicopter successfully hoisted six crab fishermen from their sinking boat 70 miles northwest of Cold Bay. The 125-foot-long *Nowitna* lost power in rough weather and began taking on water around four o'clock in the morning. That's when the skipper requested assistance from the Coast Guard.

Fortunately for the ship's crew, the Coast Guard had prepositioned its cutters and aircraft in preparation for the Opelio Tanner crab season. The effort, known as Operation Northern Safeguard, strategically places

A member of the Coast Guard's elite Tactical Law Enforcement Team fastropes from a Jayhawk. This insertion technique is often used to quickly board a ship at sea. *U.S. Coast Guard*

A Jayhawk helicopter and small craft from the Coast Guard cutters *Farallon* and *Manitou* assist with the rescue of more than 300 migrants stranded on Flamingo Cay after their boat went aground. *U.S. Coast Guard*

assets in the Bering Sea and Bristol Bay to limit the loss of life by ensuring that helicopters and surface ships can quickly reach a crab boat in trouble. When the *Nowitna* called for help, a Jayhawk helicopter, a C-130 airplane from Air Station Kodiak, and the Coast Guard Cutter *Mellon* were quickly deployed.

Coast Guard crews battled 40-knot winds and 20-foot seas during the five-hour rescue mission. Using the Jayhawk's external winch and rescue basket, the crew chief and rescue swimmer managed to carefully hoist the fishermen from the sinking vessel. The rescue hoist has a 200-foot cable and can lift 600 pounds at a time. All the men were subsequently flown ashore, examined by doctors, and then released with a clean bill of health.

The flight deck officer on the medium-endurance cutter *Campbell* (WMEC-909) guides an HH-60J Jayhawk in for landing. Unlike navy ships, which have their helos approach the landing deck from the rear right quadrant, Coast Guard cutters have their helicopters approach directly from the rear. *U.S. Coast Guard*

A Jayhawk lands on the helo pad of an offshore lighthouse. There are hundreds of navigational aids off the coast of the United States that the Coast Guard is responsible for maintaining, ranging from buoys to lighthouses. The Jayhawk was designed to perform in violent storm-force winds up to 63 knots and exceptionally heavy sea states. *U.S. Coast Guard*

Drug Interdiction

Stopping the flow of illegal drugs into the United States from outside sources is a challenge, to say the least. That's because there are some 300 ports of entry into the United States, with more' than 400 million people entering or reentering the country each year, plus 157,000 boats, 585,000 airplanes, and 128 million cars. Drugs are shipped overland from adjacent countries, shipped directly to U.S. ports concealed in containers, flown into the country via couriers on commercial airlines or in private aircraft, or are air-dropped to waiting ships in the Caribbean for shipment to U.S. markets.

When it comes to busting drug smugglers on the high seas, the Coast Guard is in charge. It shares that responsibility with the U.S. Customs Service, however, if it involves drug runners trying to sneak into the country using a plane.

To hunt down smugglers in the so-called Transit Zone—a six-million-square-mile expanse of water that includes the Caribbean, Gulf of Mexico, and eastern Pacific Ocean—the Coast Guard works closely with the Drug Enforcement Administration's El Paso Intelligence Center, the CIA's Counternarcotic Center, various Department of Defense field assets (e.g., ground radar, aerostats, patrol aircraft), Department of State, and

Aircrew help offload $80 million worth of cocaine seized from a hidden compartment aboard the 200-foot motor vessel *Anne* in the Bahamas. The Coast Guard works with other federal agencies in patrolling six-million square miles of ocean for drug smugglers. *U.S. Coast Guard*

"Cozy" is the word to describe the working environment of a Jayhawk. Here an Avionics Technician (AVT) monitors the helicopter's systems. He holds the position of flight mechanic when part of an aircrew and is responsible for maintaining and repairing the Jayhawk's power, communications, navigation, auto flight, and sensor systems. *U.S. Coast Guard*

several joint task forces that collect intelligence information. When a suspicious target is detected, the Coast Guard launches its cutters, patrol boats, and aircraft to intercept it. These assets are often accompanied by aircraft from other federal agencies.

The Jayhawk helicopter is ideally suited for this type of mission, since it can use its dash speed (180 knots) to catch up with the smuggler. It also has the ability to land on narrow strips of sandy beach, hover directly over a ship, and transport and embark heavily armed boarding teams. Furthermore, its pilots can use night-vision goggles to track smugglers in the dark.

In late October 2002, two Jayhawk helicopters from Air Station Clearwater played a role in a major drug bust on Grand Bahamas Island. A U.S. Customs surveillance aircraft flying over the Caribbean had initially detected a suspicious "go fast" speedboat and notified the Coast Guard. For the next 16 hours, the Customs plane provided air coverage tracking the 32-foot-long "go fast" as it zigzagged between shoals, reefs, and islands, and sped across open water.

In the middle of the night, the speedboat finally made landfall, and the suspects scrambled out and fled into the forest on foot. Just as quickly, the first Coast Guard Jayhawk helicopter landed on a nearby beach and unloaded its law-enforcement team, which consisted of two DEA and Bahamian Drug Enforcement Unit officers. Shortly afterward, a second Jayhawk arrived on the scene and aided in the search. Eventually, three of the four suspected drug runners were captured and arrested.

Lieutenant James Knapp, aircraft commander of the first Jayhawk on-scene, stated that night-vision goggles were vital in detecting and tracking the "go fast" and were especially important during the confined-area landing on the beach.

After sunrise, the 18 bales of cocaine—worth $10 million on the street—and the three prisoners were loaded into the Jayhawks and transported to Nassau, Bahamas.

Space Shuttle Security

Since 1981, the Coast Guard has provided security and search-and-rescue capabilities for more than 300 unmanned space launches and every single space shuttle mission. In the hours before a launch, the Coast Guard Marine Safety Office in Jacksonville, Florida, establishes a

An HH-60J Jayhawk patrols the skies over New York City in the aftermath of the September 11, 2001, terrorist attack. While air force fighter jets conduct combat air patrols high above to defend Manhattan from aerial attack, the Jayhawk keeps a close eye on so-called targets of opportunity on the ground that terrorists might want to attack, such as piers, bridges, pipelines, symbolic monuments, and petroleum storage tanks. *U.S. Coast Guard*

maritime security zone around the Kennedy Space Center to keep boaters at a safe viewing distance and thwart any potential terrorist attack. This zone is patrolled by planes, helicopters, and up to 20 patrol boats of various sizes.

Additionally, the Coast Guard prepares for any accident that might happen during the launch phase of the space shuttle. Personnel from the Coast Guard Seventh District command center in Miami stand by at Patrick Air Force Base in Florida to assist with search-and-rescue planning in case the astronauts have to bail out during liftoff.

To date, two memorable space shuttle events have involved the Coast Guard. The first occurred on January 28, 1986, when space shuttle *Challenger* exploded 73 seconds after liftoff. Helicopters from Air Station Savannah flew nearly 19 hours on 8 sorties between January 31 and February 5 while assisting in recovery operations. Although the Coast Guard did not have any Jayhawk helicopters at that time, the disaster does reveal the role the service would play today if such a disaster happens again. It was one of the largest

The rescue hoist is the most commonly used device to extract survivors from the ocean or a boat. Although the Jayhawk is equipped with a 200-foot-long cable capable of lifting 600 pounds, pilots prefer to stay below 70 feet when rescuing someone. Higher altitudes cause the hoist to swing and rotate, creating a potentially dangerous situation for the survivor and the helicopter's crew. *U.S. Coast Guard*

to Alexandria, Louisiana, and 230 miles (north to south) from Sulphur Springs, Texas, to metropolitan Houston.

The Coast Guard immediately placed its units on standby—including Jayhawk helicopters—to assist FEMA and NASA with transportation and recovery efforts. The service also issued a warning to boaters in the region—including those on the Gulf Coast—to report any debris found to local law-enforcement officials and not to touch the objects, since they might have been contaminated with hazardous chemicals.

Right: Rescue swimmers practice a search-and-rescue extraction technique during a training exercise off Elizabeth City, North Carolina. On December 17, 2002, a Jayhawk helicopter set a new record when it rescued 26 crew members of the M/V *Sea Breeze I* after the 600-foot, Panamanian-flagged passenger ship began to sink some 290 nautical miles east of Cape Charles, Virginia. The helo is designed to carry six passengers plus the four crew. In this rescue, three times as many people were aboard. *U.S. Coast Guard*

search efforts in history, with searchers recovering more than 12 tons of shuttle debris while scouring 150,000 square miles of ocean surface.

The second tragedy happened on February 1, 2003, when space shuttle *Columbia* disintegrated during its reentry back to earth—just 16 minutes from its scheduled landing time at the Kennedy Space Center in Florida. Debris from the *Columbia* was strewn in an area stretching 380 miles (west to east) from Eastland, Texas,

Whitehawk

VH-60N Specifications

Crew: Four—pilot, copilot, crew chief, communication system operator
Seating: Configurable; up to 10
Rotor diameter: 53 feet, 9 inches
Height: 16 feet, 10 inches
Fuselage length: 50 feet, 11 inches
Overall length: 64 feet, 11 inches
Fuselage width: 7 feet, 9 inches
Fuselage ground clearance: 1 foot, 7 inches
Turning radius: 41 feet, 8 inches
Engines: Two General Electric T700-401 C gas turbines
Speed: 184 mph (maximum); 167 mph (maximum cruise)
Range: 360 miles with 30-minute loiter

Depending on whom you ask, the Whitehawk earned its name for one of two reasons: its distinctive white-painted top or because the bald eagle—the symbol of America—is a quasi white hawk. Regardless of which story you favor, this helicopter is flown by the Marine Corps' Executive Flight Detachment of Helicopter Squadron One (HMX-1) to transport the president and other senior officials, as directed by the White House Military Office.

While the craft outwardly resembles the army's original Black Hawk—color scheme aside—the Whitehawk is entirely different inside. As an executive transport helicopter, it features customized seating plans with plush leather reclining seats, air conditioning, handcrafted carpeting, and exterior electric steps that slide in and out for passengers to use when entering or exiting.

If you look closer, you may notice that the main cabin features enhanced soundproofing as well as bulletproof windows and doors. But only the most observant will note that the Whitehawk is shielded from the electromagnetic pulse of an exploding nuclear bomb, that it carries an integrated GPS/Flight Incident–Cockpit Voice Recorder and a plethora of infrared countermeasures and electronic warfare systems to thwart incoming missiles, and that it is equipped with advanced, highly survivable, jam-resistant communication systems (e.g., MILSTAR, DSCS, Mystic Star) that enable the president to communicate with the nation's military commanders anywhere in the world and to send and receive top-priority messages.

The Marine Corps has eight of these birds under its control, solely for presidential and VIP transport. The VH-60N Whitehawks are maintained by the Executive Flight Detachment at two facilities: Marine Corps Air Facility Quantico in Virginia and Anacostia Naval Station in Washington, D.C.

Quantico serves as the main headquarters for HMX-1, while Anacostia is a forward, self-contained detachment for emergency relocation of the president and top government officials to either an underground command post—such as Site R in Raven Rock, Pennsylvania, or Mount Weather in Bluemont, Virginia—or an awaiting E-4B National Emergency Airborne Command Post Boeing 747 aircraft. (Such an evacuation event is codenamed Crown Helo.) The Anacostia-based Executive Alert Facility is a restricted-access compound staffed by HMX-1 marines. It features hangars, helicopter landing pads, a 500-foot runway, living quarters, underground fuel storage, fuel trucks, and aviation ground-support equipment.

Only two helicopters are approved to fly the president of the United States: the SH-3 Sea King (*top*) and the VH-60N Whitehawk (*bottom*). The Whitehawk has seating for 10 passengers, and the aircrew consists of a pilot, copilot, crew chief, and communication system operator. The helo can be folded quickly (in less than two hours) for loading and transport on an air force C-5A Galaxy or a C-17 Globemaster III. When the president is aboard, the helicopter's call sign is Marine One. *HMX-1/U.S. Marine Corps*

History of "The First and Finest"

Helicopter Squadron One was established in December 1947 as an experimental unit to test and evaluate helicopters and tactics for the Marine Corps. On September 7, 1957, President Dwight D. Eisenhower was vacationing at his summer home in Newport, Rhode Island, when he was suddenly required to return to the White House. Typically, such a trip meant an hour-long ferry ride across Narragansett Bay to Air Force One at the airport, followed by a 45-minute flight to Andrews Air Force Base and a 20-minute motorcade ride to the White House.

Realizing this was inexpedient for the situation at hand, Eisenhower ordered an aide to find a faster way to get him to Air Force One. The aide informed the president that an HMX-1 helicopter was on station in Rhode Island in case of an emergency and could fly him to the plane. The president liked the idea and took a historic 7-minute trip to the airport in the UH-34 Seahorse.

Soon thereafter, HMX-1 was asked to evaluate the feasibility of landing a helicopter on the South Lawn of the White House. Once test flights proved that it could be done safely, HMX-1 began flying the president to and from the White House to Andrews Air Force Base, the home of Air Force One. This service was initially shared with the U.S. Army, but in 1976 the Marines were assigned the sole responsibility of providing helicopter transport to the president of the United States, vice

A Whitehawk lands on the lawn of the White House. The Marine Corps' Helicopter Squadron One (HMX-1) responds directly to the White House Military Office's requests to transport dignitaries. Distinguished Visitor Code 1 (DV-1) missions are exclusively for the president, while DV-2 missions include the vice president, cabinet members, chief justice, service secretaries, members of congress, and the directors of the CIA and FBI. Civilian Code 2 missions are rare and usually involve a specific task, such as a U.S. Senator visiting a counternarcotics operation in the Caribbean. *HMX-1/U.S. Marine Corps*

president, secretary of defense, secretary of the navy, commandant of the Marine Corps, and all visiting heads of state in the Washington, D.C., area.

Today, HMX-1 (also known as Nighthawks) is comprised of more than 700 personnel. While most of the squadron is involved in testing aircraft and developing helicopter tactics, the Executive Flight Detachment is dedicated to presidential transport and is supported by 63 officers and 149 enlisted men in operational and fleet support activities. The detachment is often referred to as White Side—in reference to the paint scheme for the tops of the helicopters. It is also known as the Cage, since all helicopters and materiel are kept behind a security fence.

The VH-60N Whitehawk is in high demand, with the squadron logging over 11,300 flight hours annually. In presidential election years, that figure increases. To date, the squadron has not experienced any mishap during a presidential lift mission.
HMX-1/U.S. Marine Corps

Marines assigned to operate and maintain the VH-60N—which replaced the aging VH-1N in 1988—are selected from the Marine Corps' existing pool of aviation personnel and have no previous experience on this helicopter. That's because there is no official military occupational specialty for presidential pilot.

The most qualified candidates are actively sought out and recruited for HMX-1. They spend up to a year with the squadron, learning the basics on the Green Side (i.e., everything outside the Cage) while undergoing a background investigation. Once they are given appropriate access and clearance—Top Secret and Yankee White—from the Department of Defense, White House Military Office, and the Department of the Navy, they are eligible for transfer to the White Side. This process is so stringent that 15 to 20 percent of assigned personnel fail to qualify, and hence, must leave the squadron. Only 13 positions within HMX-1 do not require a security clearance.

All pilots must have more than 1,500 hours of flight time to be eligible for HMX-1, although this requirement may be waived on rare occasions where an individual demonstrates superior airmanship. The 2,000-flight-hour requirement for the White House Helicopter Aircraft Commander role, however, cannot be waived.

Until late 2002, HMX-1 pilots used flight simulators located at Naval Air Station Jacksonville, Florida, because HMX-1 did not have access to its own aircraft simulators. Hence, pilots received training in standard-fleet SH-60 Seahawk and SH-3 Sea King simulators before commencing with the VH syllabus, which includes courses on the Whitehawk's airframe, powerplant, controls, indications, communication, navigation, and countermeasures systems. Pilots also undergo on-the-job flight training.

Today, however, HMX-1 has a VH-60 simulator known as the Aircrew Procedures Trainer, built by Aero Simulation Inc., that enables the squadron to conduct both initial and refresher pilot training. One special feature is the RDR-1300 Weather Radar Simulation System, which provides real-time graphics and simulated radar return imagery for numerous weather patterns, targets, and landmasses that are unique to four different database regions. Using it, pilots can practice flying the Whitehawk through thunderstorms in mountainous terrain—or any other environment they are likely to encounter in real life.

The commanding officer (CO) of HMX-1 is required to be a colonel, a naval aviator or a naval flight officer, and must have served with HMX-1 as a pilot. A prospective CO spends a year with the squadron learning the ropes and undergoing extensive training before finally assuming command. During his two-year tour, the commanding officer oversees the entire squadron and ensures that the emergency evacuation mission (at both the Anacostia facility and on the road with the president) is always ready to execute, and he serves as the presidential helicopter pilot. As such, he pilots Marine One, the call sign for the helicopter that has the president onboard.

Five other Marine One–designated pilots can step in to fly a presidential helicopter. Any other helicopters in the flight, transporting White House staff, Secret Service personnel, or journalists, are assigned a call sign of Nighthawk 2, Nighthawk 3, and so on. Nighthawk 2 is always the same type helicopter as Marine One, while Nighthawk 3, and others are CH-53 or CH-46 Green Side aircraft.

On the Road

The Whitehawk is ideal for overseas assignments on short notice, since its main and tail rotor blades, stabilator, and tail rotor pylon fold easily for loading onto an air force C-5 Galaxy, C-17 Globemaster III, C-131 Hercules, or C-141 StarLifter aircraft. The marines in the Cage can prepare a Whitehawk for loading in less than two hours.

The air force strategic airlifters are provided by the U.S. Air Mobility Command to transport the president and are referred to as Phoenix Banner missions. (Airlift missions for the vice president are codenamed Silver, while those for the Secret Service are called Copper.) For presidential trips abroad, HMX-1 pilots fly the Whitehawks to Andrews Air Force Base, where they are dismantled and loaded aboard C-5 Galaxys, which subsequently transport them to a forward operating base. A C-5B Galaxy can carry up to three helicopters.

When on a mission, the HMX-1 detachment is completely self-contained, supported by dedicated aircrew, maintenance, technical representatives, security personnel, and logistics for the duration of the event.

HMX-1 officers assigned to the White House Liaison Office plan the squadron's logistics for all presidential trips and brief the detachment before each mission begins. The Plans Department at Quantico manages the classified planning portion of each presidential trip, such as arrival times and emergency landing zones. The Nighthawks' Security Department provides armed security at the squadron's facilities and at every trip site where the Whitehawks are used. This mission alone requires more than 200 military police and counterintelligence personnel on a worldwide basis.

Once the HMX-1 detachment arrives at its destination, the Whitehawks are reassembled and undergo a post-maintenance inspection flight. Additionally, each helo is given a five-hour penalty flight to ensure that all systems are working properly. Finally, any helicopter selected to fly the president or other dignitary must conduct exact rehearsals one day prior to the event.

Handled with Kid Gloves

As can be expected, the VH-60N Whitehawk receives meticulous care that exceeds normal standards to keep the aircraft in superior condition. After all, this helicopter flies the leader of the United States. It can never be allowed to have a bad day.

On the routine side, the Whitehawk is washed weekly to meet HMX-1 standards. It is also wiped down by hand (a task called ragging) after every flight, inspected for corrosion, and lubricated and serviced after every 150 hours of flight time. A major overhaul of the aircraft occurs every 28 months or 2,400 flight hours, whichever comes first. The maintenance, upgrade, and rebuild process are done at Sikorsky, inside secure portions of the plant. All supplies for the Whitehawk are in a closed-loop system, meaning everything is marked, monitored, and kept within the VH inventory for reissue on Whitehawk helicopters only. Doing so limits the possibility of sabotage and espionage.

When components are refurbished by Sikorsky or prime contractors, they are returned to blueprint tolerances instead of to rework tolerances, unlike normal aircraft parts. All parts of the Whitehawk are replaced at 75 percent of their life expectancy. This ensures the reliability of the helicopter when it comes to transporting the world's leaders.

The VH-60N Whitehawk has a service life of 10,000 flight hours, which means it will remain in service until about 2015. As that date approaches, a determination will have to be made whether to replace the Whitehawk or extend its life by an additional 10 years through a Service Life Extension Program.

The space shuttle *Discovery* lifts off from the Kennedy Space Center on a mission to resupply the International Space Station. Since the advent of the space shuttle program in 1981, the U.S. Coast Guard has been tasked with providing security and search-and-rescue capabilities. The Jayhawk has played an active role in that endeavor. *NASA*

CHAPTER FIVE

FLYING INTO THE FUTURE

The MH-60R Strikehawk (also known as Romeo) carries active/passive sonobuoys as well as the airborne low-frequency sonar (ALFS). As a multi-mission anti-submarine-warfare helicopter, it needs to be able to detect subs in both the outer and inner zones of the torpedo exclusion area established around an aircraft carrier battle group. The sonobuoys are ideal for quiet listening, while the powerful ALFS dipping sonar aggressively searches out a submarine's hiding place among the noise produced by a fleet of ships. *U.S. Navy*

As the previous chapters have illustrated, the Black Hawk helicopter has successfully metamorphosed over the past 25 years to fill nearly every niche a helicopter possibly could—from moving soldiers around the battlefield to persecuting submarines at sea and from rescuing civilian survivors and military prisoners of war to transporting the president of the United States around the globe. Simply put, there has never been a more flexible helicopter design in history.

One would think that after such a stellar career the future would hold little promise, since the helicopter has essentially "been there, done that." But that's not true. The future of the Black Hawk is, in fact, brilliant. The navy is currently revolutionizing its helicopter fleet. By the year 2020, the service intends to replace eight existing helicopter designs with just two—the new MH-60R and MH-60S.

The MH-60R, referred to by some as Strikehawk, will replace the SH-60B Seahawk, SH-60F CV Helo, and HH-60H Combat Support Helicopter. It is a multi-mission helicopter that will be able to conduct undersea warfare, anti-surface warfare, and anti-ship surveillance and targeting missions, as well as logistics support, naval gunfire fire support, and search-and-rescue. To achieve these roles, the MH-60R—or Romeo, as the letter R is called in the military—will feature an advanced multimode radar system, integrated self-defense system, low-frequency sonar, and major upgrades to its acoustic processor and avionics suite. The navy expects to acquire 241 MH-60R helicopters over the next 15 years.

Visually speaking, the Romeo looks like the Seahawk. For example, it retains the large radar antenna dome under its chin as well as the 5x5 sonobuoy launch matrix on the left side. What is noticeably different is the addition of a FLIR sensor on the nose and the Airborne Low Frequency Sonar (ALFS) transducer on the underside of the fuselage.

ALFS is an acoustic system that enables the crew to detect and track technologically advanced submarines, whether they are in deep or shallow waters. Like the AQS-113F dipping sonar it replaces on the SH-60F, ALFS is lowered into the water by cable. But when it reaches the desired depth, it unfolds to three times its normal size, increasing its aperture threefold. Using low-frequency pulses (below 5 kHz), the system provides greater detection ranges of submarines. In fact, tests have shown that ALFS offers three to six times more capability over the existing 113F system.

Another remarkable advancement for the Romeo is its multimode radar (MMR), which features Inverse Synthetic Aperture Radar. This system automatically tracks up to 255 contacts simultaneously. It identifies each target not just as a ship or aircraft but, more impressively, as to specifically what type, class, and capability.

Furthermore, the MMR allows the helicopter to detect a submarine's periscope when it is used. This is an amazing feat, especially when one considers that periscopes are small targets and are exposed above water for a very short time. How the MMR actually accomplishes this is classified, but it is likely the system relies on laser-imaging radar (LIDAR) technology. Rather than using radio waves, LIDAR uses laser beams—projected either continuously or in bursts at a higher repetition rate—to determine the location, distance, and speed of an object. Since laser is more concentrated than a radio wave, it provides a clear, high-resolution image. Hence, a

This strange-looking vessel is a high-speed experimental catamaran built for the navy and army to transport nearly 400 troops and combat equipment—including Black Hawk helicopters and 30 to 40 Stryker fighting vehicles—into forward areas. The *Joint Venture* (HSV-X1) was deployed for military operations in Kuwait during Operation Enduring Freedom in February 2003. In this photo, a brand new MH-60S Knight Hawk approaches the ship's flight deck. The helo, which has a larger cabin area for cargo and passenger transport, will be used for a variety of missions, including underway replenishment. *U.S. Navy*

submarine's periscope could be easily discerned, even if exposed only for several seconds. The laser would indicate that the periscope, unlike a bird, lacks wings and sticks straight up out of the water.

Low-rate initial production of the MH-60R Strikehawk has already begun, and the helicopter is being vigorously tested. In February 2003, while undergoing evaluation at the navy's Atlantic Undersea Test and Evaluation Center off Andros Island in the Bahamas, the helicopter successfully located a submarine using ALFS while simultaneously conducting a radar sweep of the ocean surface for hostile ships and

aircraft using the multimode radar and electronic surveillance measures (ESM). This milestone was important, since it proved that the radar, acoustics, and ESM systems worked together, just as they should in a real-world environment.

The other helicopter being introduced into the navy is the MH-60S Knight Hawk. It replaces the HH-1N, SH-2G, SH-3H, and CH-46 helicopters as a fleet combat-support helicopter capable of vertical replenishment, medical evacuation, executive transport, range support, humanitarian assistance, and amphibious search-and-rescue. It will also support

An MH-60S Knight Hawk assigned to the providers of Helicopter Combat Support Squadron 5 (HC-5) flies past the guided-missile destroyer USS *John S. McCain* (DDG-56). The Knight Hawk shares the same night-vision-goggle-friendly digital cockpit configuration with the new MH-60R version, which enables pilots to fly either helicopter. The "glass" cockpit provides the pilot and copilot each with two 8x10-inch active-matrix liquid-crystal screens—a flight display and a mission display. *U.S. Navy*

the navy SEALs in overwater missions and will eventually replace the MH-53E Sea Dragon as an airborne minesweeper.

The Knight Hawk is essentially an army Black Hawk body configured with the navy Seahawk's engines, rotor system, and dynamics, including the Seahawk's automatic rotor-blade folding system, folding tail pylon, improved gearbox, rescue hoist, rotor brake, and automatic flight-control system. The Black Hawk's battle-proven airframe provides the Knight Hawk with greater cabin volume and double sliding-door access, which facilitates cargo transport as well as rapid troop entry and debarkation.

The rugged airframe design also enables the helicopter to use the army's External Stores Support System, which

means the SEALs have a variety of weapons and fuel tank options to support them in carrying out a mission. This includes mounting laser-guided Hellfire missiles, 70mm aerial rockets, and various gun pods.

Additionally, the helicopter's tailwheel has been moved farther to the rear. This permits steeper and more aggressive landings in confined areas—an environment in which the SEALs typically operate.

The Knight Hawk's low-infrared reflective-paint scheme and engine-exhaust venting system reduce the helicopter's infrared signature, making it difficult for heat-seeking missiles to target it. The MH-60S also has provisions for a laser detection system, a missile plume-detection system, a radar warning receiver, an active infrared-jamming system, and chaff and flare dispensers. Combined, these help the helicopter crew detect and thwart incoming threats.

During Operation Iraqi Freedom in 2003, American fighter aircraft dropped hundreds of bombs on Baghdad. This photo shows an MH-60S Knight Hawk transporting free-fall bombs from an ammunition supply ship to the flight deck of the aircraft carrier USS *Constellation* (CV-64). The Knight Hawk's external cargo hook can easily transport up to 9,000 pounds. The bombs appear to be Mk-82 500-pound general-purpose bombs—sans fuze and tailfin assembly, of course. *U.S. Navy*

The most difficult challenge for the Knight Hawk is turning it into a minesweeper. It is simply too small to tow the heavy minesweeping sleds used by the MH-53E Sea Dragon, which has 30,000 pounds of tow tension. (By contrast, the Knight Hawk has 6,000 pounds of tow tension.) Hence lightweight sleds that trigger mines to explode by contact, acoustics, or magnetic fields are being designed for the Knight Hawk. The helicopter will also be able to tow a side-looking sonar system to detect mines. In practice, since a helicopter can tow only one item at a time, two helicopters will work in tandem during minesweeping missions. One helicopter will tow the sonar to search for mines, while the other tows a sled to detonate any mines found.

The Knight Hawk is also equipped with LIDAR, which enables the crew to locate mines on the bottom or suspended from the bottom of the ocean. Since the deepest draft for ships is 40 to 50 feet, the LIDAR apparently has the capability of penetrating at least that depth of water.

To ensure the destruction of mines, the navy is considering two options. The first is an armed robot (also known as the Airborne Mine Neutralization System) deployed by the Knight Hawk after a mine has been discovered by sonar or LIDAR. The wire-controlled robot runs around on the bottom of the ocean, goes up to a mine, and blows itself up—just like a suicide bomber. The second option is mounting a Mk-44 30mm gun inside the cabin of the Knight Hawk. When a mine is discovered in shallow water, the 11-foot-long gun is used to blow it up. Engineers, however, are still puzzling over what the effects of the tremendous recoil will be on the helicopter's airframe.

The navy intends to procure 237 Knight Hawks. The prototype was flown in 1997 and approved in 1998 for low-rate initial production. The first squadron to fly the aircraft was Helicopter Combat Support Squadron 3 (HC-3) Packrats in October 2001.

The navy is not the only military service relying on the Black Hawk series of helicopters in the future. The army continues to have a love affair with the Black Hawk as well. In fact, it is embarking on the UH-60M program, which will remanufacture 1,217 aging UH-60A and UH-60L helicopters into a standardized configuration, so they can remain in service through 2025. The upgrade replaces the old needle-and-dial cockpit with a modern, digitized cockpit with multifunction displays and improves the helicopters' lift, range, maneuverability, and safety. It will also enhance a pilot's situational awareness on the battlefield. The UH-60M is scheduled to enter army units in 2006.

Way down the road is the UH-60X program. Referred to as the Future Utility Rotorcraft (FUR), the UH-60X is conceptual at this point, but the army recognizes that it needs an advanced and more capable helicopter around 2012. Some of the things the army would like in this helicopter include the ability to lift 10,000 pounds in a hot-and-high-altitude environment, a cruise speed of 200 mph, a flight radius of 575 miles, increased survivability against crashes and enemy weapons fire, and a 20 percent handling improvement over the present UH-60L Black Hawk.

While these features sound challenging or, in some instances, even far-fetched, realize that when the army issued its wish list for the follow-on generation of helicopters after the UH-1 Iroquois in the late 1960s, the Black Hawk was born. Given American ingenuity and technology, it should surprise no one that the UH-60X will indeed become reality. When it does, it will be the king of all the Hawks, thoroughly dominating the airspace, as its cousins have for a quarter century.

A sailor assigned to the combat stores ship USNS *San Jose* (T-AFS 7) attaches a hoist line to an MH-60S Knight Hawk helicopter as it prepares to deliver cargo to the aircraft carrier USS *Kitty Hawk* (CV-63) during Operation Iraqi Freedom in 2003. While the primary role of the Knight Hawk is cargo transport, its large cabin can be easily reconfigured with roll-on/roll-off modular kits to meet the needs of the mission at hand, whether it is evacuating medical patients, inserting/extracting a SEAL squad, transporting palletized cargo, or hunting and detecting mines. *U.S. Navy*

GLOSSARY

AAA: Anti-Aircraft Artillery. Referred to as "Ack-Ack" or "Triple A" by pilots.

Bandit: Any aircraft positively identified as being hostile.

Bat turn: Pilot slang for an extremely sharp turn or bank.

Bent gun: A brevity code meaning a weapon has malfunctioned or is unsafe to use until further notice. This code is followed by the gun position, i.e., "Bent gun, left side."

Bird farm: Nickname for an aircraft carrier.

Bogie: Any aircraft not positively identified as friendly.

Bogie dope: Brevity code meaning, "I need information on an unidentified target or aircraft."

Chaff: A passive form of electronic countermeasure used to deceive airborne or ground-based radar.

Close trail: Two or more aircraft staggered one behind the other.

Combat control team: An elite U.S. Air Force unit that precedes the main body of an airborne assault force to provide guidance to incoming aircraft, using beacons, infrared devices, radio, and other equipment.

Drop point: A point within a landing zone where helicopters are not able to land because of the rough terrain but in which they can unload cargo or soldiers while in a hover.

Element: A flight of two aircraft.

Fast mover: Slang for a military jet.

Feet dry: Aircraft is over land.

Feet wet: Aircraft is over water.

Flight: Formation of two or more aircraft.

FLIR: Forward-Looking Infrared, an imaging device that translates thermal sources (i.e., infrared) into a visual picture. It is widely used on helicopters, enabling pilots to fly low and fast at night in all terrain and weather conditions. Pronounced "fleer."

Gofast: Nickname for a vessel moving at more than 20 knots. In drug interdiction missions, it generally refers to a high-speed cigarette boat.

Hangar flying: A lively conversation among pilots and aircrew as they recall, describe, and compare—in great detail—some of their combat flight encounters and missions.

Hangar queen: Slang for an aircraft that never seems to get out of the hangar, either because it is in need of repair or because it is habitually scavenged for spare parts for other aircraft.

Helicopter ambush: Any of several methods used to ambush and destroy an incoming helicopter to a landing zone (LZ) and/or prevent troops from disembarking. For example, placing a mine with a friction fuse in a treetop adjacent to the LZ, so that the downdraft created by the approaching helicopter detonates the weapon, resulting in shrapnel being sprayed skyward.

HIFR: Helicopter In-Flight Refueling. *See* **Hot pump.**

Hostile: A radar or visual contact positively identified as being the enemy.

Hot: A brevity code meaning that an area, landing zone, or objective is receiving—or is expected to receive—enemy gunfire.

Hot pump: Slang for a Helicopter In-Flight Refueling (HIFR), a technique by which a helicopter hovers over a ship while being refueled.

Jinking: An aircraft maneuver in which the pilot abruptly changes the flight path of the aircraft in all planes at random intervals. It is usually used to avoid a gun attack.

Joker fuel: The amount of fuel required to accomplish a mission and return via the planned route with reserve.

Judy: A brevity code meaning, "I will take control of the intercept; no more assistance is needed."

Lock-on: Target is being automatically tracked by radar. *See also* **Tracking.**

MANPAD: Man-Transportable Air Defense. In other words, a surface-to-air antiaircraft missile, such as the Stinger. Such missiles pose a significant danger to helicopters.

No joy: A brevity code meaning that the helicopter's aircrew does not have visual contact with the downed crew member, target, team, or landmark. *See also* **Tally.**

Ops check: A periodic check of an aircraft's systems (including fuel) by the aircrew to ensure everything is safely functioning as it should.

Padlocked: A brevity code meaning that the aircrew cannot take their eyes off the downed crew member, target, team, or landmark without the risk of losing visual contact.

Pararescuemen (PJ, pararescue jumper): In the air force, an elite group of volunteers who are skilled medics and rescue experts. They administer first aid to wounded aircrewmen under combat conditions.

Platform: A brevity code used by a gunner to request that the helicopter's altitude be changed because the present altitude does not allow the weapon to hit the target.

RESCAP: Rescue Combat Air Patrol.

Sanitize: To clear an area of threats.

Scramble: Take off as quickly as possible.

Slime lights: Nickname for the formation lights used by Black Hawk helicopters during nighttime operations. The intensity of the lights is adjusted as required to provide sufficient illumination and outline the proceeding aircraft.

Sort: To distinguish friendly aircraft from suspect or known hostile aircraft.

Spaghetti: Pilot slang that refers to the line drawings representing an air combat maneuver.

Tally (Tally ho): A brevity code meaning that a downed crew member, target, team, or landmark location has been positively identified in relation to the helicopter. The code is followed by a clock position and a distance. *See* **No joy.**

Time on target (TOT): Specified time at which the aircraft is either on the ground or established in a hover and ready to perform the required mission (e.g., insertion, survivor pickup).

Tracking: The act of locking a radar or infrared sensor onto a target.

VERTREP: Vertical replenishment, the resupplying of ships at sea using helicopters. The provisions are slung beneath the helicopter in a special cargo net.

White top: Nickname for a VH-60N Whitehawk used to transport the president of the United States. So named because of the helicopter's distinctive white color scheme.

WOPS: Water operations.

INDEX

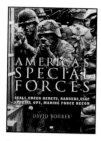

America's Special Forces
ISBN 0-7603-1348-2

U.S. Air Forces Special Ops
ISBN 0-7603-0733-4

U.S. Army Special Forces
ISBN 0-7603-0862-4

**U.S. Elite
Counter-Terrorist Forces**
ISBN 0-7603-0220-0

Modern U.S. Navy Destroyers
ISBN 0-7603-0869-1

Marine Force Recon
ISBN 0-7603-1011-4

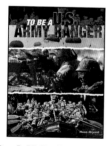

To Be A U.S. Army Ranger
ISBN 0-7603-1314-8

**AWACS and Hawkeyes:
The Complete History of
Airborne Early Warning Aircraft**
ISBN 0-7603-1140-4

**Lockheed Secret Projects:
Inside the Skunk Works**
ISBN 0-7603-0914-0